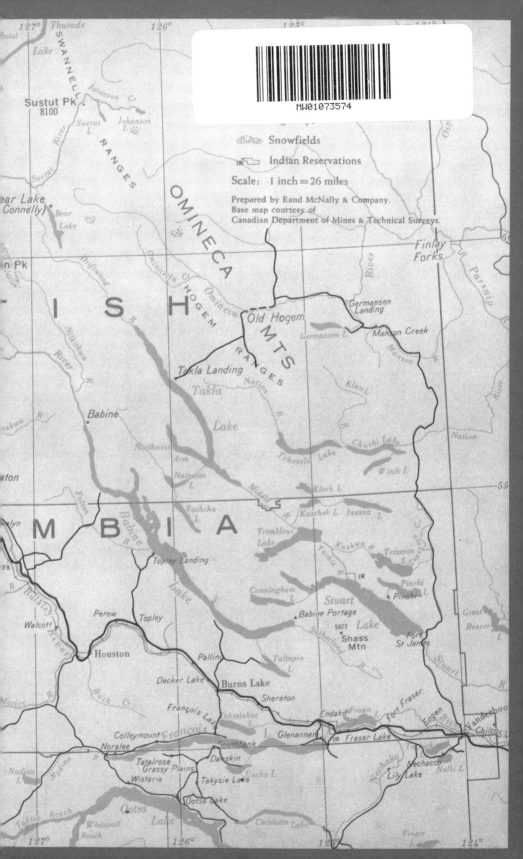

Author playing 13-pound steelhead on lower bay of Johanson Lake

STEELHEAD
PARADISE

PUBLISHING NOTE:

Steelhead Paradise was originally published in 1963 and needless to say, many things have since changed in the steelhead paradise of British Columbia. The biggest change has been the growth of catch and release which was necessary to preserve stocks of wild steelhead, for there are no hatchery-run steelhead in the Skeena River watershed. Catch and release was necessary because of the commercial net interception of the target fish (salmon) and consequent large incidental catch of steelhead trout near the mouth of the Skeena River. In some years this incidental commercial catch of steelhead is about 50% of the total run and if anglers also were allowed to kill steelhead the spawning population would be seriously impacted. For that reason catch and release regulations have been strongly supported by anglers.

Since 1972 I have fished most of the rivers author John Fennelly wrote about. They are all fine rivers offering wild steelhead in beautiful surroundings. Several of these rivers are being heavily sport fished today and for that reason the government of British Columbia is considering regulations to modify fishing pressure.

I particulary enjoyed this book because of its pioneering nature concerning steelhead fly fishing and that is why I decided to re-publish it. Many of my most cherished fly fishing moments have occurred on the streams inside this book and it is a very warm feeling indeed, to know that because of wise fisheries management the wild steelhead of the Skeena and Nass river systems should continue to propagate themselves naturally and in good numbers far into the future.

Frank W. Amato, 1989

STEELHEAD PARADISE

by John F. Fennelly

FRANK AMATO PUBLICATIONS
P.O. BOX 82112
PORTLAND, OREGON 97282

John Fennelly had an unusual and varied career. He graduated from Princeton in 1920 with a Phi Beta Kappa Key — and the welterweight boxing championship of the University. Thereafter he was successively a newspaper reporter, employee in a grain firm, associate editor of a financial magazine. He acquired a Ph D from Princeton, and for two years taught economics at Columbia University.

Fennelly entered the investment business in 1929 and became a partner of Glore, Forgan & Co. in 1935. In addition to his main activity in the investment business, he was a director of Libby, McNeill & Libby, Abbott Laboratories, Stewart-Warner Corporation, and Champlin Oil and Refining Company.

In World War I he served as a flying cadet in the United States Army Air Corps. During World War II, he was on the staff of the War Production Board in Washington where he functioned as Director of the Program Bureau and Vice-Chairman of the Requirements Committee which made all the basic allocations of essential war materials.

In addition to having published numerous articles on economics and finance, John Fennelly was co-author of a book published in 1942 by the National Bureau of Economic Research entitled *Fiscal Planning for Total War.*

Acknowledgements

I AM INDEBTED to several of my friends for the photo-graphs from which the illustrations for this book were made. All of the excellent black and white photographs were taken by Buzz Fiorini. The several illustrations in color were the work of Brian Magee, Gus Craig, Hal Hentz, and Hunter Perry. I am deeply indebted to George A. Poole, president of Poole Bros. Inc., for technical assistance in the preparation of the illustrations, and to Walter Nietschmann, cartographer of Rand McNally & Company, for producing the beautiful map shown in the end pages. My daughter, Anne Fennelly, assisted materi-ally in making many helpful suggestions for revision of the manuscript. Finally, I am indebted to my wife for her encouragement and unfailing patience in bearing with me during the writing and rewriting of the book.

JOHN F. FENNELLY

Table of Contents

Illustrations

Foreword

I F YOU are a dedicated fly fisherman you are also a dreamer of
dreams. Often on cold winter nights you lie awake and conjure up
the perfect wilderness trout stream. On the gin clear water of this dream
river you place your tiny dry fly with delicacy and precision, and
every second or third cast produces the savage strike of a huge fish.

Unfortunately very few present day anglers find in real life anything
that bears resemblance to their dreams. With automobiles and hard
surfaced roads encroaching steadily upon our remaining wilderness areas,
the great majority of fly fishermen must be content to follow in the
wake of hatchery trucks on overcrowded streams.

Nevertheless, there are still a few remote areas on the North American
continent where fly fishing comes close to the vision of the dedicated
angler. One of these is the valley of the Skeena River in northwestern
British Columbia. It has been my good fortune to visit this
country on six separate occasions during the past decade in pursuit of
the great steelhead trout that inhabit its many beautiful streams. I
know of no area in the world today where one can find steelhead in
such large numbers, and of such great size. One of the last frontiers
where fishing of this kind is still available, it is truly a paradise
for stream fishermen.

Although every fisherman on the Pacific Coast is familiar with the
nature and habits of steelhead there are many eastern anglers who
know little or nothing of this magnificent game fish. It seems desirable,

therefore, to dispose at this point of the question—"What is a steelhead trout?"

In simplest terms a steelhead is a variety of rainbow trout that migrates to the ocean as a small fish, and then returns to its native stream one to three years later to spawn. It returns many times larger and stronger, and exceeds in size and strength all but a rare few of the rainbow trout which have not migrated to salt water. When it first enters fresh water the steelhead has no rainbow coloration; its back is dark green and its sides and belly are pure silver. The longer it remains in fresh water the more the rainbow colors return to its sides, and, finally, as it approaches the spawning period, it tends to become much darker over-all than other rainbow trout.

An almost endless controversy has raged amongst fishermen as to whether a steelhead is an ordinary rainbow which happens to migrate to sea or whether it is in fact a separate sub-species of the rainbow trout. To me the problem is one of very minor importance. I am entirely satisfied to accept the evidence produced by the Fisheries Research Board of Canada which indicates that steelhead are probably a separate sub-species. Some years ago, Mr. Ferris Neave[*] of this Board collected and segregated eggs from migratory steelhead and non-migratory rainbows, then marked and released the fingerlings. The offspring of the steelhead almost invariably migrated to sea while the offspring of the resident rainbows remained in the river. Moreover, the two groups of fish showed small but consistent differences in scale counts.[†]

From a fisherman's standpoint, the really important fact is the incredible vitality of steelhead. I have caught these fish more than 400 river miles upstream from salt water and 5000 feet above sea-level. After such a journey against fast water, rapids and falls, with little or no food, these steelhead are astonishing in their endurance. On numerous occasions I have hooked twelve and fourteen pound steelhead

[*] Citation from Roderick Haig-Brown, *Fishermen's Spring*, pp 163-164.
[†] Since writing the above I have learned that early in 1959 British Columbia authorities decided to abandon a sub-species classification for steelhead. Now all types of rainbow trout are classified under the name of *salmo gairdneri*. The decision was reached on the grounds that differences between steelhead and resident rainbows are too small to justify separate classifications. If this latest development tends to add even more confusion to the situation, it also serves to emphasize the unimportance of the whole problem.

in these upper waters and had them put up battles lasting a solid hour or more, interspersed with tremendous runs and jumps before their final surrender. I have yet to meet the equal of a fresh-run or bright steelhead as a game fish.

During my six visits to the Skeena Valley I have covered most of this large watershed and have fished in practically all of the principal tributaries of the Skeena as well as in the Skeena River itself. Although it is still predominantly an area of rugged mountains and trackless forests, each passing year witnesses a gradual encroachment of civilization upon the wilderness sections of this country. Within another decade or two most of its primeval charm is certain to disappear. While there are still large areas in the Skeena Valley virtually untouched by the hand of man, it has seemed worthwhile to put down on paper some account of the beauty of the country, and the pleasures it holds for a fisherman.

Finally, this little book makes no pretense of being a treatise by an expert. It is a tale told by an amateur of some wonderful fishing experiences. Because it is a factual history, the story is a report of at least as many failures as successes. For this reason it may disappoint those readers who are accustomed to the fiction of "wrist jarring strikes", and similar flights of fancy which are the common currency of many of our popular outdoor magazines. Nevertheless, I hope my story will appeal to all genuine anglers who love to wet their lines in wilderness streams.

I *The Skeena Valley*

DEEP, AND dark with glacial silt, the Skeena River appears sluggish but has a deceptively heavy current. This big stream, with its numerous tributaries, drains many thousands of square miles of north-western British Columbia, breaks out through a gap in the coastal range of mountains, and finally empties into the Pacific Ocean near the seaport city of Prince Rupert.

The Skeena Valley lies roughly between the 54th and 57th parallels and stretches eastward more than 250 miles from the ocean. North of the Skeena Valley is the valley of the Stikine River which also flows into the Pacific, and the watershed of the great Mackenzie River which finds its outlet in the Arctic Ocean. Immediately to the south lies the watershed of the Fraser River which, after a long and tortuous course, empties into the Pacific at Vancouver some 500 miles farther south.

My first glimpse of the Skeena watershed was from the cabin of a Grumman Goose plane on the Saturday morning before Labor Day, 1951. I was one of a party of five flying in from the coast with Stanly Donogh of Seattle, who was owner and pilot of the plane. Our group had chartered Donogh's 78-foot houseboat for a three-week cruise north along the wildly beautiful coast of British Columbia. On board the plane from the boat were Bill Bacon, Wesley Dixon, Stuart Templeton and myself. In addition, Stanly had picked up our friend, Jack Kellogg, at his summer home on Saltspring Island and brought him along for the trip.

Stanly and Jack had flown up the evening before and joined our boat at River's Inlet. The plan was to fly us over the coastal mountains for a long weekend of inland fishing on the Babine River. Saturday morning, to our dismay, found the whole coastline socked in with a heavy fog. This problem, however, did not stop our friend, Stanly Donogh. He announced that he would taxi us along the coast in the plane in the hope of finding a hole in the fog bank through which he could ascend.

We climbed aboard and started up the coast. About an hour later Stanly spotted a break in the fog bank and took off immediately. Spiraling upward through the opening we emerged into brilliant sun-shine at about 6,000 feet. Except for a few craggy peaks of the coastal range which thrust their snow-capped heads up through the overcast, nothing was visible at any distance but an unbroken sea of clouds.

Although the subject was never mentioned, the same gnawing worry was in each of our minds. What if we should find the same solid cloud layer on the eastern slope of the mountains? How could Stanly bring the plane down in this rugged, unknown country? For the next half hour as we flew inland the cabin was full of nervous laughter and feeble attempts to crack jokes.

Suddenly we looked down and saw below us green forests and sparkling lakes. It was a beautiful sight for all of us. The sudden break in the tension expressed itself in a rush on the primitive toilet facility which we carried. Although we did not realize it at the time, we were now over the Skeena Valley flying in a northeasterly direction along the line of the Morice River.

The source of the Skeena River lies in rugged mountain country close to the 57th parallel. For the first 200 miles it follows an irregular course southward until it reaches the town of Hazelton. At this point the Skeena turns to the southwest and flows another 200 miles before it empties into the Pacific Ocean at Prince Rupert.

Inside the cover is a map which shows the network of streams which make up the Skeena watershed. The three principal tributaries which join the Skeena above the town of Hazelton are the Kispiox, the Babine, and the Sustut. The Kispiox enters the Skeena a few miles northeast of Hazelton after an irregular course from the northwest. The Babine and

Morice Lake

Morning mist on Sustut Lake

Sustut rivers flow into the Skeena from the east about 50 and 100 miles respectively north of Hazelton.

Beautiful Morice Lake lies in the southwestern corner of the Skeena watershed and is surrounded on three sides by the coastal range of mountains. Morice River originates in Morice Lake and flows some fifty miles to the northeast until it joins the Bulkley River at the little village of Houston. The Bulkley then follows a course to the northwest for about 100 miles before it empties into the Skeena at Hazelton.

The flow of water from Morice Lake, which is 2,600 feet above sea level, travels about 400 miles and describes almost three-quarters of a complete circle before entering the ocean. Sustut and Johanson Lakes, in the northeastern corner of the watershed, also lie approximately 400 river miles from the ocean. Sustut Lake, where the Sustut River rises, is 4200 feet above sea level, while Johanson Lake, some twenty-five miles to the northeast, has an elevation of almost 5000 feet. Johanson Creek, which originates in Johanson Lake, joins the Sustut River about six miles below Sustut Lake.

Except for a few isolated Indian villages, the only settlements in the Skeena Valley are a string of small towns and villages spread out along the east-west route of the Canadian National Railway. How complete a wilderness most of the area was only twenty-five years ago is vividly described in that charming book, "Driftwood Valley" by Mrs. Theodora Stanwell-Fletcher. Shortly before World War II, Mr. and Mrs. Stanwell-Fletcher spent two full years on the Driftwood River north of Takla Lake, and the book is a delightful account of their experiences.

During the past few years, however, motor roads have been edging gradually out into the wilderness. When I first visited Morice Lake in 1951 there was no road within fifty miles. Since then a road has been opened up to the lake and was completed in 1958. When I first fished the Kispiox in 1954 a motor road followed the stream about fifteen miles up from its junction with the Skeena. On my return in 1959 I found the road had been extended for another twenty-five miles up the river. In 1954 a road was opened from Hazelton to the Babine River. More recently a road was built between the town of Smithers and the west side of Babine Lake.

Nevertheless, there are as yet no roads north of the Babine River. As a result, vast areas in the northern part of the Skeena watershed remain as untouched by civilization as was the Driftwood River country twenty-five years ago. The only access to this rugged mountain country is by pack horse or float plane. For the hunter or fisherman this area is still a virgin wilderness.

The spectacular coastal range of mountains, capped with eternal snow and many glaciers, divides the watershed into two distinct parts. Marked differences in climate and vegetation exist between the eastern and western slopes of these mountains. On the western side of the range the proximity of the Pacific Ocean produces very heavy rainfall and prevents extreme fluctuations in temperature. Thus, at the town of Ketchikan, located at the southern tip of Alaska and only a short distance north of Prince Rupert, the annual rainfall averages close to 180 inches. The forests on the western slope, therefore, are similar to those on the Olympic Peninsula in the State of Washington— huge fir, spruce and cedar trees with an undergrowth of luxuriant ferns.

East of the coastal range, however, the rainfall, while abundant, is much less heavy, and the temperature in winter drops as low as 50 to 60 degrees below zero, Farenheit. The result is that the forests contain very few large trees and consist mainly of slender lodge-pole pines.

Although lacking the majesty of huge trees, the Skeena Valley east of the coastal range has great scenic beauty. Most of its lakes are surrounded by heavily wooded and snow-capped mountains. Its many streams, except for the Skeena itself, are fast flowing and very clear when the water is reasonably low. For many years I was certain that Morice Lake was the most beautiful body of water I had ever seen. It is thirty-five miles in length, and is surrounded on the south, west and north by the coastal range, which rises in this area to a top elevation of 9,000 feet. Not only is the lake itself entirely uninhabited, but when I last visited Morice Lake in 1955, the nearest human habitation was the little village of Houston about 50 miles to the northeast.

Now that I have seen Johanson and Sustut Lakes, I am forced to admit that these two much smaller bodies of water are at least equal in beauty to Morice. Johanson and Sustut are both surrounded by spectacularly beautiful mountain ranges. Johanson Lake, with an elevation above sea level of over 4800 feet, lies just above the timber line, while Sustut is about 600 feet lower.

Indelibly etched in my memory is a scene witnessed late one night at Johanson Lake. Our party was lodged in a small log cabin on the south shore of the lake. Directly opposite, and almost due north, a mountain range rose almost sheer from the water's edge to a crest some 2000 feet above us.

Awaking about one a.m., I thought I heard the sound of wolves and went outside to listen. Every star in the sky was visible, and a full moon had just edged above the rim of the mountains in the east. Small patches of snow on the range acrosss the lake caught the moonlight and shone like polished silver. The lower half of the mountain still lay in shadow—not black, but deep purple in color.

Shooting skyward from behind the range were six separate beams of Northern Lights. They spread out in the shape of a fan, and brought to mind the rays of the rising sun on the Japanese flag. These shafts of light were white and unwavering. Two of them were so brilliant that it was hard to believe they were not produced by huge military searchlights directly behind the crest of the range.

Not a breath of air stirred. From all points of the compass came the baying of timber wolves. I say "baying" because the sound was very different from the mournful song those wolves give forth in the dead of winter. It was a prolonged deep bark, repeated endlessly in regular slow cadence.

Before the twenty degree temperature drove me back to the cabin and the warmth of my sleeping bag, I had time to contemplate the problems which would face a landscape artist attempting to do justice to this scene. If he saw it through eyes like mine, the result would certainly cause critics to accuse him of being melodramatic and unrealistic. I finally concluded that the picture called for the talents of a Maxfield Parrish, whose overly dramatic and sentimental paintings served as illustrations for many of the books of my childhood.

Just before I fell asleep, another thought entered my mind. How singularly appropriate it was that this magnificent display of the Aurora

Borealis should have appeared from behind the range opposite our camp. For this particular range forms part of the divide between the Skeena watershed and that of the Mackenzie River. Thus, every drop of water that trickles down the other side of this mountain eventually finds its way into the Arctic Ocean. In my imagination I could picture these great beams of light flashing across the arctic tundra and the barren lands of the Northwest Territories, and finally being turned skyward by our mountains. A fanciful vision, of course, but pleasing to contemplate.

THE FISHING SEASON

Because of topographic and climatic conditions, the fly fishing season on most of the streams in the Skeena Valley is relatively short. During the summer months until about August 15 the run-off of snow from the mountains is very heavy. The result is that most of the rivers are flooded and discolored with glacial silt. About the middle of August the run-off is checked by colder weather, and the streams drop rapidly. For example, I have watched the Morice River drop several feet during the last two weeks of August.

As the water levels drop and the streams clear, the trout fishing improves and reaches its optimum just before the salmon start spawning. This usually occurs at varying dates between the 1st and 15th of September. The great enthusiasm of rainbow trout for salmon eggs dulls their interest in artificial lures, and trout fishing slows down materially. While fishing in the Morice River close to spawning salmon, I have actually seen a line of rainbow trout ten to fifteen feet downstream waiting for the eggs to drop from the female salmon.

By the end of September the salmon spawning is usually ended and all the salmon are either dead or dying. Trout fishing now picks up again and remains excellent as long as the weather permits. Although I have never remained in the Skeena Valley after the first of October, I understand that steelhead fishing is usually better in October than in September.

The main problem is the weather. In the mountainous northern part of the watershed one is likely to be snowed in or frozen in by the middle of October. My friend, Buzz Fiorini, was isolated at Johanson

Lake for the last two weeks of October one year by a sudden freezing of the lake. He and his companion, Mac Anderson, were very lucky to get out at all. A rescue plane on floats flew in on the first of November and fortunately found enough open water at the upper end of the lake to land and take off.

Farther south late fall fishing is less dangerous but increasing rain and cold are likely to make the sport somewhat less pleasant. Jack Nelson, our head guide on the Morice River, has written me of fishing the Upper Morice around the middle of November. After closing the camp on the lake, Jack with his partners, Barry and Martin Grainger, drifted several miles down the river from the outlet of the lake, fishing as they went. The weather was wet, cold, and thoroughly miserable. Nevertheless, they had strikes from rainbow trout on almost every cast, the fish taking dry flies as readily as wet. Jack wrote that he had never seen such good fishing in his life.

Buck Morris, my taxi-driver guide from Smithers, has written me of wonderful steelhead fishing in the Bulkley River in the middle of December. Somehow the idea of wading in a stream in December at 55 degrees north has never aroused my enthusiasm.

Just a few words about insects. I understand that during July and August mosquitoes and black flies are troublesome throughout the Skeena Valley. Early in August however, with the coming of the first frosts, these pests disappear rapidly. I can say truthfully that I have never been bothered by insect bites between the middle of August and the first of October.

STEELHEAD AND SALMON RUNS

Steelhead trout spawn late in the winter and in early spring, usually during February, March, and April, and then return to the ocean in the late spring.* Fresh steelhead start straggling into the Skeena during July and early August. These summer runs are relatively light and sporadic. About the middle of August the heavy fall runs of steelhead commence, and continue without interruption until well into January.

* Les Cox, game warden at Smithers, has written me that he has seen occasional steelhead spawning as early as November and some as late as May. He agrees, however, that most of the spawning occurs in February and March.

Most authorities divide steelhead runs into only two classifications: summer-run and winter-run fish. In terms of these categories, a high proportion of the steelhead that enter the Skeena tributaries during the fall should be classified as summer-run fish. The problem is really one of the relative sexual maturity of the fish rather than of the actual time of their entry into fresh water. The steelhead that run into rivers many months in advance of their spawning are usually sexually immature. These fish are bright in color and retain most of the behavior characteristics of the resident rainbows. These are the typical summer-run steelhead, regardless of whether they are found in streams in August or in October.

The typical winter-run steelhead, on the other hand, is well advanced toward sexual maturity, is darker in color, and reacts quite differently to fishing lures than do the summer-run fish. These different characteristics are discussed more fully in later chapters. At this point it is only pertinent to note that most of the steelhead found in the Kispiox River in late September are typically winter-run fish because of their advanced state of sexual development. On the other hand, most of the steelhead found in the Sustut and Johanson rivers at the same time of the year are typically summer-run fish.

A considerable but undetermined percentage of steelhead survives the spawning period and some actually return later to their native rivers to spawn a second time. Immediately after the spawning the fish are in a weakened condition and are highly vulnerable to attack by predators. Further attrition of their number takes place in the long return trip to salt water. They are then subject to all the uncertainties and vicissitudes of life in the ocean. The result is that relatively few are able to return to fresh water and spawn a second time. According to studies made by the Game Commission of British Columbia, less than ten percent of the steelhead come back to their native rivers for a second spawning.

The Skeena River system provides one of the greatest spawning grounds for salmon in western Canada. All varieties of Pacific salmon enter the Skeena. These are: the big king or spring salmon, which run in weight from 30 to over 100 pounds; the cohoe, or silver salmon which run from 3 to 30 pounds; the small humpback salmon, known as "humpies"; the sockeye or red salmon, which are the most valuable commercially, and generally run from 3 to 8 pounds; and finally the dog salmon, known commercially as chum.

Although all of these types come up the Skeena, wide differences are found in the choice of spawning grounds by the several varieties of salmon. The cohoe is the only type I have found in every one of the tributaries of the Skeena that I have fished. In the Morice one sees only king and cohoe salmon; the Babine has one of the biggest runs of sockeye salmon in western Canada; humpies provide the chief run on the Kispiox, with smaller runs of cohoe and dog salmon. I have seen only cohoe salmon on the Sustut and Johanson Rivers.

Unlike Atlantic salmon and steelhead trout, all Pacific salmon die immediately after spawning. In fact, the process of disintegration is already well advanced by the time these fish reach their spawning grounds. In this stage the hump-back salmon turns almost black while all other types turn bright red. Except for the cohoe, Pacific salmon will rarely take a fly. This is fortunate because they are not fun to catch and rarely fit to eat by the time they have reached the spawning area.

I have hooked a considerable number of cohoe salmon in the upper streams with wet flies. These have usually been fairly bright fish and, therefore, still good to eat. Occasionally these cohoe will put up short but spectacular battles. I hooked a 15 pound cohoe on the Upper Sustut River that jumped six times and ran like a steelhead, but then was beached in less than fifteen minutes.

Fly fishing for cohoe in or near salt water is a very different matter. Using a fly rod and a large streamer fly floated on the surface, trolling for cohoe off the coast of British Columbia can be great sport. These fresh cohoe are magnificent fighters and provide as good eating as any fish I have ever tasted.

King salmon will occasionally take a wet fly when they first enter fresh water but I have never seen or heard of one taking a fly in the upper water at or near their spawning grounds. They will, however, take a large spoon, probably striking at it in anger rather than from any desire to feed.

Occasionally, for the sake of variety, I have fished for king salmon on the Upper Morice with a plug casting rod or a spinning rod. When one of these big fish took the spoon, a long tedious battle followed, without jumps or long runs, and usually ended in a victory for the salmon. Once when casting from a boat anchored in midstream a gigantic king salmon followed my spoon right up to the boat, practically bumping it with his nose as he approached. He was so huge that he looked like a submarine. He was at least five feet in length, and must have weighed somewhere between 80 and 100 pounds. I actually breathed a sigh of relief when he finally turned away. I understand that fishing for king salmon near tidewater is an exciting and strenuous sport but in the upper streams it is boring and thoroughly unprofitable.

II *The Morice*

DURING THE YEARS when I fished it between 1951 and 1955, the Morice was the closest approach to the dream river of a dedicated fly fisherman that I ever hope to see. A big stream with fast flowing current and crystal-clear water, it had an almost endless series of beautiful pools for many miles below the lake.

An unbroken pine forest pressed hard on the banks of the river. The trees were so uniform in size and stood so close together that the Morice appeared shut in from the outside world by high stockade walls. The brooding silence of these woods was almost oppressive, an effect which was heightened by the complete absence of any songbirds. The only sounds were the raucous cries of ravens wheeling overhead, and the shrill piping of a young bald eagle from its nest in the top of a dead pine. Also on rare occasions, one would hear some unseen, heavy animal crashing through the dense undergrowth behind the blank wall of trees.

I had never heard of the Morice until I first saw it from the air on the Saturday before Labor Day, 1951. As described in the preceding chapter, our party of five flew in that morning from the coast with Stanly Donogh in his Grumman Goose. After clearing the coastal range we followed a beautiful river for many miles in a northeasterly direction. From our maps we learned it was the Morice. It looked so attractive for fly fishing that we decided to try it on our way back to the boat.

After two days of good but not spectacular fishing on the Babine

River we headed back for Morice Lake. Stopping to gas up at the Smithers Airport we made numerous inquiries about fishing on the Morice. To our surprise, however, we could not find a soul who knew anything about it, although the lake was less than one-hundred air miles distant. We touched down on Morice Lake shortly after noon on Labor Day and taxied to shore about one-hundred yards from the outlet to the river.

Almost immediately after our flies hit the water all five rods were in action with large rainbows. None of us had ever seen anything like it, and the excitement was intense. I remember seeing Bill Bacon charge several hundred yards down the bank in an effort to keep up with a wildly leaping three pound trout, and the sight made me wonder about the condition of his heart. The action kept up steadily until three p.m., when we had to break off in order to get back to the boat before dark. After returning at least a dozen fish to the stream, we carried on board the plane 18 rainbow trout weighing a total of 45 pounds.

These were the brightest and firmest trout we had ever seen. The only break in the silver sheen of the scales was a thin faint line of rainbow color along each side. Another interesting fact was the uniformity in size of these trout. Almost invariably they ran somewhere between a minimum of two pounds and a maximum of four pounds. A similar observation was made by Edward Hewitt in his account of fishing the Yellowstone River in the 1880's. He noted that practically all the trout weighed between two and four and one-half pounds* and stated that "evidently this was the natural population of the river at that time, when it had not been disturbed by fishermen".

In 1951 our party used nothing but wet flies, mostly streamers. We were all so imbued with the tradition of using dry flies only in warmer water that it occurred to none of us that trout would rise to dry flies in the 45 degree temperature of these northern rivers. Jack Kellogg, however, had noticed a lone fisherman on the Babine who cast beautifully and used nothing but dry flies. Jack was sufficiently intrigued to attempt dry fly fishing when he returned to the Morice with Stanly Donogh in 1952 for a weekend of fishing. He then

---

* Edward R. Hewitt: *A Trout and Salmon Fisherman for Seventy-five Years*, Charles Scribner's Sons, p. 16.

discovered the important fact for all of us who fished this stream in subsequent years, that the Morice River rainbows would take dry flies more readily than wet flies, despite the low temperature of the water.

After our brief but thrilling experience on Labor Day, we decided to return the following Saturday and spend the weekend camping beside the river. The second visit, however, proved a severe anti-climax. Huge king salmon were spawning all over the river and we learned for the first time that, when salmon eggs are available, trout show little interest in artificial lures. We all caught a few rainbows but, as compared with the preceding Monday, the fishing had slowed down to a walk. It was fascinating, however, to watch the spawning of the big red salmon. They ignored us completely. On several occasions while wading in fairly shallow water male salmon almost brushed against my legs as they charged about driving away rivals from the nests of their mates.

My one piece of good fortune that weekend was meeting Jack Nelson, and Barry and Martin Grainger who served as guides on all my later visits to the Morice. The meeting had an amusing aspect. As we taxied toward the shore after landing on the lake, I was stationed in the nose of the plane as a lookout for sunken logs. We were all certain there was not another soul within at least 50 miles. As we came up to the beach, however, we saw a large boat emerge from the mouth of the river. On board were seven men. They landed and came marching along the beach toward us. All seven had heavy growths of beard and each man carried a high-powered rifle.

The same thought occurred simultaneously to each member of our party: "My God, this must be a band of outlaws about to take us over." Instead, to our great relief, they turned out to be a big game hunting party of four radio executives from Topeka, Kansas, accompanied by the three guides mentioned above.

We saw no steelhead in the Morice in 1951, although several of our party lost flies on very heavy strikes from fish which remained unseen. In fact, none of us dreamed of finding steelhead some four hundred river miles up from tidewater. When I took my first steelhead on the Upper Morice two years later the event came as a complete surprise not only to me but to our guides as well.

My next visit to the Morice was in August of 1953. This time I was accompanied by John Harlan (now Mr. Justice Harlan of the United States Supreme Court) and Charlie Smyth, professor of chemistry at Princeton. We entered the Morice River some fifty miles below the lake and spent five days moving slowly upstream against the heavy current in Jack Nelson's big river boat. Several times we had to help the heavy boat up through rapids, clinging desperately to its gunwales while wading waist-deep in icy water. You could not help wondering what might happen if you should lose your grip in that racing torrent.

The river was still very high and we found no good fishing until we reached the mouth of Gosnell Creek about ten miles below the lake. It is interesting to note that this was the first fishing party that our guides had ever taken up the river. All of their previous expeditions had been with big game hunters. I believe, in fact, that we were the first group of fly fishermen ever to ascend the Morice River.

We reached Morice Lake on Saturday, August 15. The water was still high but dropping rapidly. The fishing improved daily and was simply magnificent for the two weeks of our stay at the lake. We used practically nothing but dry flies, mainly Wulff deer-hair flies, on Nos. 8, 10, and 12 hooks. We took so many good rainbows that almost immediately we adopted the practice of flattening the barbs on our hooks so as to return the fish uninjured to the stream.

Our trip was marred by one near tragedy and one real tragedy. On the way up the river John Harlan began to get sick and by the time we reached the lake was too ill to go out and enjoy our first day of really good fishing. By a very fortunate coincidence my friend, Donogh, flew in that same evening to set up a camp for three men who were cruising off the coast with their wives in Stanly's houseboat.

All that Saturday night John was violently ill. Just as dawn was breaking I followed him out of the tent and sat with him for a while on a log in almost freezing temperature. I told him he must fly back that afternoon with Stanly to Seattle; otherwise, he might never get out of the country alive. John agreed reluctantly. He flew to Seattle with Stanly, returned to New York by air the next day, and spent an entire month in a hospital recovering from a bad stomach ulcer.

The following Wednesday evening Stanly Donogh flew in again

with his three guests from the boat. When we visited their camp the next morning I noticed that their only means of water transportation was a small aluminum boat which Stanly had brought in by plane. We offered to take some of the party in our big boat down the lake to the mouth of the river about two miles distant. Fred Whiting of Chicago was the only one dressed for fishing so we took him with us. We put him ashore just above the outlet to the river with the understanding that the others would join him in about fifteen minutes. Just as we left to fish farther downstream I told Whiting that he would find good fishing around the point where the lake swept in a big curve into the river.

When Stanly and his two other guests reached the foot of the lake a short time later Whiting had disappeared. They found only his small tackle bag hanging from the branch of a tree on the bank. After a fruitless search by all of us for the rest of the day, Stanly flew out to the town of Burns Lake to report the accident. He brought back with him a corporal of the Mounties and the local game warden.

These two men, along with our three guides, found Fred Whiting's body two days later in 12 feet of water and about a half mile downstream from the lake. Also recovered was his landing net with a fly and the end of a leader caught in the mesh. From this bit of evidence we concluded that Fred was probably in the process of landing a fish when he slipped off into the heavy current and was drowned. It was a grim and depressing affair and gave me renewed respect for the power of these big turbulent rivers of the north.

The very next day I encountered my first steelhead in the Morice. I was fishing alone in a large pool about five miles below the lake. My attendant guide, Barry Grainger, sat on the bank with his 30-06 rifle across his knees as an ever present protection against grizzlies.

Wading well out into the stream, I was casting a dry fly into the edge of the current which swept in a semicircle around the quiet water of the pool before emptying out into a long rapids below. The fly was a No. 12 Royal Wulff on a 2x nine foot leader. My rod was a 4½-ounce nine-foot Leonard and my reel was a small one, with only sixty yards of backing behind the fly line. For the two to four pound resident rainbows of the stream this tackle had been adequate.

On my casts across the large pool my fly would float beautifully around the arc of the semicircle and then be pulled under briefly by the drag of the line at the foot of the pool. Just as the fly started to drag across the current on one of these casts, I felt a heavy strike and found myself fast to what I thought was a large rainbow. The fish fought hard but I was successful in keeping it in the pool and out of the rapids below. Within about ten minutes I managed to work the trout into the quiet water and soon had it on the beach. My de-liar registered just over five pounds, which made it the largest rainbow I had landed on the river.

A few minutes later I was casting a fresh No. 12 Royal Wulff across the pool. At exactly the same spot, just as the drag started in front of a large sunken boulder, I felt another heavy strike. One second later, the largest fish I had ever seen on the end of my fly line erupted three or four feet into the air. I yelled at Barry to be sure he had seen the monster. His back had been turned, however, and he did not see the first tremendous jump. When he saw the second, he shouted: "Jesus! Mr. Fennelly, it's a whale."

At this point my big fish turned suddenly downstream and was off like an express train into the rapids with my line and backing screaming out from my reel. Since it was impossible to follow down along the shore, I was certain the fish was lost. I quickly lowered my rod tip and pointed it downstream, my only thought being to save the rod when the impending break should occur. The accidental result, however, was to put some slack in my line which gave me my only possible chance of stopping such a heavy fish in a downstream rush.

With only a few feet of backing left on my reel the fish turned and charged upstream at high speed. It was already back in the middle of the pool before I was able to recover all of my slack line. Then followed thirty minutes of short rushes back and forth across the pool with several more jumps. I waded out to the limit of my chest waders at the foot of the pool and thus managed to keep the fish above me and out of the rapids below. I had to play it very gingerly because of my light leader, and over forty-five minutes elapsed before it came slowly into shore on its side. Barry slipped my small net under its tail and heaved my fish out on the bank.

Without question I had a steelhead, which looked so enormous to me that I could hardly believe my eyes when the scale showed only 10 pounds. The fish had perfect rainbow coloration slightly darker in hue than our usual smaller rainbows. Comparing the big fish with the five pounder landed earlier, we found both fish identical in markings and coloration and concluded that both were steelhead.

During the balance of our stay at Morice Lake scarcely a day passed that Charlie Smyth and I failed to tie into one or more good steelhead. We landed about twenty of these fish, from 4 to 10 pounds. All were taken on dry flies. The eagerness with which they rose to a dry fly is illustrated by one experience with a fish which I eventually lost.

Since my first meeting with steelhead, I had shifted to larger tackle. I was now using a 5¼-ounce, 9½-foot Powell rod and a Hardy St. John reel which carried two hundred yards of backing. On this occasion I was casting toward the shore from our boat which was anchored in midstream. A sudden heavy rise took place under my fly which was drifting about 25 feet away. I struck and missed the fish. The strike jerked the fly back toward me, and it lit on the water with the line lying in a tangle around it. Instead of being frightened, the big fish charged in at once and took the fly solidly not more than five feet from the boat. It then bored straight upstream, the run ending in a big jump at least two hundred feet above me.

The fish then turned and went tearing downstream. We pulled anchor and drifted down after it. About fifteen minutes later, and a quarter of a mile downstream, my line went slack. I reeled in and found the No. 10 hook broken off clean at the shank.

One evening I was standing in shallow water nursing a nine pound steelhead back to vitality just before releasing it. I had gone ashore from the boat in order to beach the fish, and our head guide, Jack Nelson, was watching quietly from the boat close by. He suddenly exclaimed: "Mr. Fennelly, you and Dr. Smyth are the first men I have ever seen returning fish to a stream. You know my living depends on the animals and fish of this country, and I have reached the point where I actually hate to see them killed. The only thing I have against your fellow countrymen is the large number of fish and game hogs who come here from the United States."

In late August of 1954, I returned to Morice Lake for two weeks in the company of Hunter Perry and Hal Hentz. I came back again in September of 1955, this time accompanied by Smith Richardson, George Bates, and my seventeen year old son, Dick. On both of these trips my earlier experiences with steelhead on the Upper Morice were repeated. Although the number of fish landed in each of the later years was somewhat less than in 1953, all but one of these steelhead were taken on dry flies.

Although I have since had better steelhead fishing in other streams, the steelhead fishing on the Upper Morice had a quality about it which made it as thrilling as any angling I have ever done. This was the totally unexpected character of each steelhead strike. I have never been able to spot steelhead lying in pools in the Morice, and then proceed to cast deliberately to them, as I have done elsewhere. We were always fishing the Morice for the resident rainbows which gave us constant activity. Then all at once would come a heavy strike and the tremendous jump of a steelhead, or suddenly you would see your line cutting swiftly across the current in the unmistakable first rush of one of these big fish.

One drawback about fishing for steelhead in streams where there are relatively few resident trout is that one may cast for hours, even days, without having a strike. The same, of course, is true of Atlantic salmon fishing. This tiring feature, of course, can be offset by the thrill of seeing a bunch of steelhead lying in a pool and then drifting a fly down toward them. While it is hard to beat the excitement of actually seeing a large steelhead detach itself from the school and dart arrowlike at your fly, I am afraid I still prefer the thrill of an unexpected steelhead strike as I have experienced it on the Upper Morice.

Just as in 1951 and 1953, we had excellent rainbow fishing during our entire stay in 1954. In 1955, however, we flew into the lake on September 5th and found the salmon spawning already under way. As a result the trout fishing was generally poor. Oddly enough, though, there were occasional days when the fishing would suddenly improve for no apparent reason. I remember particularly one morning when both George Bates and Smith Richardson were too discouraged to leave camp. My son, Dick, and I set out with Jack Nelson in the big

Autumn colors at lower bay of Johanson Lake

Johanson Lake under mantle of September snow

boat. We spent the day drifting several miles down the river, anchoring the boat and fishing each good pool. My bag for the day was sixteen good rainbows (all returned) and Dick's was twelve.

On the same trip occurred the most unusual coincidence of my fishing career. I was casting into the river a short distance below the lake. On one of my back casts my fly was caught in the branch of a tree behind me. After considerable maneuvering I managed to yank it free and started to examine the fly for possible damage. To my amazement, I found that my fly had pulled out of the tree another dry fly with a small bit of leader. This fly was old and bedraggled and consisted of a bunch of long black hackles. The odds against this happening even on a heavily fished stream would be enormous, but on a wilderness river like the Morice the odds must have been astronomical.

Somewhat facetiously I decided to treat this old fly as a good luck symbol, and to try fishing with it. After a few casts I had a rise and was fast to a good rainbow (about 2½ pounds). On its first run this fish wrapped itself around a snag and broke off. Muttering a few curses about good luck charms in general, I put on a fresh fly and started casting again. About twenty minutes later I had a second strike in almost exactly the same spot as the first. This time I managed to land the fish. I could hardly believe my eyes when I bent over to extract my fly from the trout's jaw, and saw the old black fly hanging from the other side of its mouth. I had to hook the same fish twice in order to prove the potency of my charm.

I spent considerable time on the Upper Morice examining the aquatic insect life of the river. Abundant fly hatches took place at irregular intervals throughout the day, ranging in size from tiny midges to large salmon flies. I remember particularly seeing a quiet section of the river literally covered with a hatch of olive duns, looking for all the world like a huge fleet of tiny sailboats. The water all around was boiling as the trout rose en masse for a hearty meal. It seemed clear that the abundance of insect life in the river was a prime cause of the large trout population in the Morice, as well as being responsible for the readiness of these fish to take dry flies.

Brief mention must be made of the other trout in the Upper Morice. Foremost among these were the Dolly Varden. These fish are a variety of char, and are speckled very much like the eastern brook trout, except that their spots are bright orange instead of pink. Dolly Varden will rarely take a dry fly and are not much fun to catch, although I have landed some as large as seven and eight pounds on wet flies. Because they prey on young rainbows and salmon fry we always killed the Dolly Varden and left them on the shore for the bears and eagles. On numerous occasions I have hooked a sizeable rainbow and then seen a much larger Dolly Varden come out of the depths and start chasing my fish. I have no love for the Dolly Varden, although it is a beautiful fish to look at when it first comes out of the water.

Also, we would occasionally catch large lake trout around the outlet of the lake by casting with a spoon. These fish were brown and speckled with whitish spots, and were known by our guides simply as char. Whether or not they are the same variety of lake trout for which the Great Slave Lake is famous, I have never tried to determine.

I feel confident that Morice Lake itself must contain resident rainbow trout of great size. The only way to find out would be to troll for these fish with a large spoon but I have never been sufficiently interested in this type of fishing to make the experiment. My friend, Gus Craig, who visited Morice Lake in 1956, caught a nine pound rainbow on a dry fly in the lake about fifteen miles up from the river and just off the mouth of a small creek. This fish was so bright that Craig was convinced it must be a resident rainbow and not a steelhead.

A family of bald eagles in a huge nest high over the river contributed greatly to the pleasure of our visit in 1954. Because the nest was directly opposite an island in the stream where excellent fishing was always found, we had ample opportunity for close observation of these big birds.

The family consisted of the two adult parents and one young eagle not quite ready to fly. Junior, as we named the young bird, fascinated us more than the adults. It was chocolate brown in color in contrast to the shiny black of its parents. Junior screeched for food all day long and was quiet only for a few moments at a time when the mother was cramming fish or other food down its mouth. Junior's appetite seemed insatiable and the poor mother spent the whole day lugging tidbits up to the nest in an effort to pacify her lusty infant. The male parent was on hand most of the time, but the drudgery of child care was obviously beneath his dignity.

We were considerably puzzled by the tremendous size of the young bird. Whenever the mother was in the nest beside Junior, the offspring appeared to tower above her. I was sure this must be an optical illusion until I read an article about bald eagles in "The Atlantic Monthly". This article stated that young eagles, just before starting to fly, are frequently larger than the adult birds. What causes them to shrink down to normal size when they start flying was not explained.

The family life of our eagles ended in stark tragedy. One day in 1954 a float plane landed on the lake and deposited two employees of an aluminum company. These men stayed for several days on the river checking the salmon runs and the water flow in connection with a possible site for a hydro dam.

One day when we stopped at our favorite island for lunch, we noticed that the nest was empty, with no sign of the eagles anywhere. Jack Nelson suspected that something was wrong and began searching the ground around the base of the big pine. He soon found some tracks leading off into the bush. He followed them and emerged shortly with the dead body of the mother eagle, shot through the heart with a heavy bullet. The wing spread of this magnificent bird was more than eight feet.

We never saw the male parent again, but we did catch a glimpse of poor Junior that evening on our return up the lake to camp. The young bird was flying clumsily from tree to tree along the shore, obviously trying to get as far away as possible from the scene of the disaster. In its state of immaturity, it was clear that this young eagle had little or no chance of surviving alone.

That evening I called on our aluminum company visitors and obtained an admission that they had shot the mother eagle. I then proceeded to tell them in no uncertain terms what I thought of such wanton cruelty, and added that such trigger-happy fools should not be permitted the use of firearms. Needless to say, we were happy to see them leave in their plane the next day.

Now that a motor road has been opened to Morice Lake, I have no desire to return. I have too many wonderful memories of the upper river when it was still in a virginal state to go back and see its banks lined with automobiles and trailer camps. Despite the heavy pounding it will now receive from hardware-throwing anglers, I believe the Morice is likely to remain a good trout stream for many years. The river is so big, and the season so short, that it will be difficult to destroy the fishing. In addition a good boat is necessary to cover the water properly, and I doubt that many of the visitors to this area will come so equipped.

THE LOWER MORICE

Jack Kellog learned from Mr. Kilpatrick of the Burns Lake Hardware store that good steelhead fishing could be found in September at the junction of the Morice and the Bulkley Rivers near the village of Houston. Mr. Kilpatrick was the expert dry fly fisherman with whom Kellogg became acquainted on our first visit to the Babine in 1951.

Early in September of 1953 Jack flew into Morice Lake to join Charlie Smyth and me and took the return trip down the river with us. When we emerged from the wilderness Charlie left us, and Jack and I spent two days fishing the lower end of the Morice. On Kilpatrick's advice, we fished a long straight run of water about two miles above the junction of the two rivers. I shall never forget the scene as we walked out to the fishing area for the first time on Labor Day morning. A heavy freeze had taken place the night before and everything was covered with a white mantle of hoar frost. Against this background the big river was startlingly blue and lovely in the early morning light.

Also on Kilpatrick's advice we used nothing but large optic streamer flies, bright red or orange in color. These flies were lightly weighted and had bright silver tinsel along the shank of the hook. Starting at the top of the run we always fished with an unvarying technique. We would cast out into the current at a slightly upstream angle. As soon as the fly hit the water we would quickly mend the line so as to permit the fly to sink deeply and to drift as far as possible downstream without a drag. As soon as the drag started, we would work the fly across the current with a slow hand-twist retrieve.

We would start off at one spot with a short cast and then gradually lengthen the line on each successive cast until we reached the limit of our casting abilities. We would then move a few steps downstream and repeat the process. We were always careful to wait until the line was straight downstream and clear of the fishable water before recovering the fly. Practically all of our fish were taken at the end of the drift as the starting drag pulled the fly up toward the surface.

In our two days of fishing Jack landed three good steelhead running from eight to eleven pounds. I landed one of thirteen pounds and lost one other. The big fish that I landed took out 150 yards of my backing and carried me a quarter of a mile downstream before I finally beached it.

When I flew out of Morice Lake early in September of 1954 with Hunter Perry and Hal Hentz, I spent three more days on the lower Morice. During the first two days I used nothing but wet flies and took three steelhead weighing from five to eight pounds. On the final day I decided to use nothing but dry flies. I was so entranced by my success with dry flies on the upper river that I saw no reason why I could not repeat it anywhere. It was a chastening experience but the beginning of my education on the diverse habits of steelhead. From early morning to late afternoon I whipped the river with every kind and size of dry fly but never had a single strike.

From local reports I learned that in both years I had fished the lower Morice about two weeks too early to meet the heavy fall run of steelhead. The first fish were apparently just beginning to come into the river early in September, and I am sure I should have had better luck later in the month when the run had reached its peak.

III   *The Babine*

ALMOST TEN YEARS were required to convince me that the Babine is one of the finest streams in the Skeena watershed for steelhead as well as for resident rainbows. One of the most baffling problems in connection with steelhead fishing in this wilderness area is the difficulty of obtaining accurate information on the timing of steelhead runs in the various streams. I have been constantly astonished by the vagueness and inaccuracy of most of the information received from local citizens. Even officers of the British Columbia Department of Fisheries have admitted that their knowledge of steelhead habits in the Skeena Valley is very limited. Their primary task is to know all about the runs of Pacific salmon, and they have little time to spend in studying a game fish like the steelhead.

What has gradually become apparent to me over the years is that each tributary of the Skeena has its own separate run of steelhead, and the time of the run on any particular tributary seems to bear little relationship to those of other streams. If one can generalize at all, it would appear that the steelhead with the longest distances to travel tend to arrive at their destinations at earlier dates than those moving upstream to tributaries which are closer to the ocean.

For example, I left the Kispiox on September 11, 1959, with the unhappy knowledge that very few of the fall run of steelhead had yet come into that stream. The very next day I flew into Sustut Lake, at least 200 river miles upstream from the mouth of the Kispiox, and found steelhead lying like cordwood in almost every pool of the upper Sustut River. Moreover, the fall run on the Morice, which like the Sustut is about 400 river miles from the ocean, seems to occur at an earlier date than the steelhead runs on the lower streams.

Another striking example of this anomaly is provided by the Babine. The junction of this stream with the Skeena is about 50 miles nearer the ocean than the point where the Sustut enters the main river. Although the Babine was the first stream that I fished in the Skeena Valley, it was only recently that I became aware that the big fall run of steelhead on this river does not get under way until around the middle of October. This is practically a month later than the peak of the run on the Sustut which is many miles more distant from salt water.

When I first flew into the Skeena Valley with Stanly Donogh early in September of 1951, the Babine was the only good trout stream we knew of. The chief reasons that the Babine was well known were the ease of landing float planes on big Babine Lake, and the availability of fishing boats at the Indian village of Babine, a few miles from the outlet to the river. Babine Lake is long and narrow, about 100 miles in length from the southern end to the northern outlet to the river. The Babine River flows in a generally western direction for some 60 miles until it joins the Skeena about 50 miles above the village of Hazelton.

We landed at the Indian village of Babine at noon on the Saturday before Labor Day and the whole population came down to the shore to greet us. At that time there were only two white men in the settlement: a Catholic priest, and the manager of the Hudson's Bay Store. Very quickly we learned that several of the Indians owned large fishing dories with outboard motors which they were pleased to rent to us for the sophisticated price of $25 per day.

That afternoon we spent about five hours fishing the lower end of the lake from the boats, and the upper end of the river on foot and in waders. Between the end of the lake and the river the Department of Fisheries had erected a fish-counting weir to keep a record of the big run of sockeye salmon that comes up the river to spawn. All along the lower end of the lake the Indians were netting and smoking salmon to provide their chief source of food for the winter months.

The rainbow trout fishing in the lower lake and in the river was good by any ordinary standards, but not nearly as spectacular as the fishing we had on the Upper Morice two days later. In all we landed about 15 rainbows running from one to three pounds. That evening we flew out and spent a very pleasant night at Douglas Lodge on Stuart Lake, about 150 miles distant.

Early the next morning we headed back for the Babine. When we came over the lake, we discovered that the northern half was covered with a heavy bank of fog. Stanly landed the amphibian on the water about 40 miles from the Indian village and started to taxi slowly down the lake. Within a few minutes, however, he was forced to cut off the engines because the fog was too dense to permit him to see any snags or floating logs that might lie in our path. For the next three hours we sat becalmed in the absolute stillness of the blanket of fog. It was a weird experience and made me glad that I did not suffer from claustrophobia.

About noon the fog suddenly lifted and we taxied rapidly down the lake to the village of Babine. Again we enjoyed a good afternoon of fishing. Although we had been advised that we would find good steelhead fishing on the Babine in early September, we saw none, nor could we learn of any steelhead that had been caught so far that year.

My only other visit to Babine Lake took place exactly ten years later in September 1961. On this most recent trip to northern British Columbia I was accompanied by my three Canadian friends, Brian Magee, Gus Craig, and Ron Sanderson. After spending two weeks exploring the headwaters of the Nass River, we decided to fly to Babine Lake for the last three days of our outing.

We pitched our camp just above the fish-counting weir, and I was surprised to find how little the scene had changed during the preceding decade. We knew that an excellent fishing lodge had been constructed some years earlier about five miles up the lake from Fort Babine. It is called Norlakes Lodge and, as we discovered two days later, provides excellent food and accommodations for fishermen. Except for this sign of encroaching civilization, the lower end of the lake, the river, and the Indian village of Fort Babine appeared wholly unchanged.

Unfortunately, we discovered we had arrived somewhat too early for good steelhead fishing and too late for the resident rainbows. Salmon spawning—chiefly sockeye and cohoe—was at a peak. Never in my life have I seen such huge masses of spawning salmon as covered the entire lower end of the lake and the upper sections of the river. It almost appeared as if one might walk across the stream on the backs of these fish without getting wet.

During two full days of fishing Brian Magee and our head guide, Buzz Fiorini, each landed two fair-sized steelhead. The rest of the party—Craig, Sanderson, and myself—had not a single strike.

When we returned to camp from the river on the evening of the second day, we became aware that the temperature was dropping rapidly. As I pulled off my wading shoes and socks I realized I would have to dry them before the camp fire unless I wished to find them frozen the next morning. Cold and hunger, however, caused me to postpone this task until after dinner. Less than an hour later, when I picked up my socks and shoes, I found them already frozen stiff.

That night the temperature dropped to 16 degrees above zero. It was the coldest night I have ever spent out in the open, and the only occasion on which I have had difficulty in keeping reasonably warm in my sleeping bag.

The next morning we all decided we had had it. That afternoon we moved bag and baggage to Norlakes Lodge where we enjoyed the luxury of hot baths, heated cabins and delicious food. After three weeks in the bush, it all seemed like heaven.

An important reason for my tardiness in learning the truth about the steelhead runs on the Babine was some official misinformation given me while fishing the upper Morice in September of 1955. We were surprised one day by the arrival of an officer of the Department of Fisheries who flew in to inspect the salmon runs on the river. During his visit we asked him numerous questions about steelhead fishing in the various streams of the Skeena watershed. Among other things he told us that the Babine was the most overrated steelhead river in the area. He advised us specifically that only 74 of these fish had been counted going through the fish weir at the foot of Babine Lake during the entire season of 1954. Since he neglected to tell us that the weir is closed at the end of September and, therefore, furnishes no record of steelhead runs after that date, I was about ready to write the Babine off as a waste of time.

Nevertheless, I took advantage of an opportunity to fish two days on the lower Babine later in that same month. When our party flew out of Morice Lake on September 17, Smith Richardson and I had arranged to stay at Hazelton for the balance of September in order to fish the Kispiox and other nearby streams.

Our guide, and an ardent fisherman himself, was Buck Morris, my taxi-driver friend from Smithers. Buck told us of a new road which had been opened to the lower Babine during the preceding year. A huge rock slide had occurred in the Babine in the summer of 1954 which had threatened to cut off the valuable run of Sockeye salmon from their spawning grounds in Babine Lake. The Department of Fisheries hastily constructed a road some fifty miles along the east bank of the Skeena from Hazelton to the mouth of the Babine and then up along the latter river to the scene of the disaster. The rock slide was blasted out in time to save the salmon run, and the road, if it could be dignified by the name, remained.

On two successive Saturdays, Buck drove us up this road to the lower end of the Babine where we fished for the greater part of each day. We found the river relatively low and crystal-clear, in sharp contrast to the high and dirty water of the Kispiox at the same time. The reason, of course, is that most of the flow of the Babine River comes from big Babine Lake where the water is always clear and the water level of which is little affected by rains. The Kispiox, on the other hand, has no big lake as its source, but originates in numerous small mountain streams. The result is that one day of heavy rain will cause the Kispiox to rise half a foot and to become heavily clouded with silt.

Despite the beautiful fishing water, we saw no steelhead on the lower Babine. The only fish we caught were several fair-sized Dolly Varden trout. By this time I was thoroughly convinced that the Babine was a total loss, at least for steelhead.

Incidentally, the so-called Fisheries highway to the Babine was, during the rainy month of September, 1955, the most excruciatingly bad piece of road I have ever attempted to travel in an ordinary automobile. How Buck Morris managed to negotiate it successfully in his Ford car I shall never understand. Everything went well, however, until we were just about six miles from the main road into Hazelton in the early evening on our second return trip.

At this point one of the rear tires went flat, and Buck made the disheartening discovery that not only was his spare tire flat, but also that he had left his pump at home.

I volunteered to walk out for help and reached the main road in pitch dark at about 8 p.m. Since it was still five miles to Hazelton I attempted to flag down each approaching car which was headed in the right direction. Three passed me at high speed but the fourth finally stopped and picked me up. It contained three men from Vancouver who were returning from a day of fishing on the Kispiox. When I expressed amazement to my new-found friends as to why the other cars had passed me up, they all laughed and replied that it was Saturday night and the other drivers must have mistaken me for a drunken Indian.

Steve Covernton, the owner of the car, proved to be the finest Good Samaritan I have ever met. He drove me into Hazelton, gave me a drink of whiskey, and then loaned me his car to carry a new tire back to my friends. I got back to Buck's car about 10 p.m. in a pouring rain. After changing the tire we finally slithered out to the main road and reached our hotel in Hazelton shortly after midnight.

The mystery of the missing steelhead on the Babine was finally solved for me by my friend Bill Fife, from Midland, Texas. I first ran across Bill fishing alone on the Kispiox when Smith Richardson and I were there in 1955. Since then Bill and I have become close friends, mainly by correspondence, although we have had two wonderful weeks of bone-fishing together off the Isle of Pines and off the coast of British Honduras.

Bill visited Norlakes Lodge on Babine Lake in September of 1956, and again during the same month in 1957 and 1958. On all three trips he had, as I would have expected, very poor steelhead fishing. Because of my own experiences and the information received from the Fisheries officer, I kept telling him I was sure he was wasting his time trying to find steelhead in the Babine.

Finally Bill wrote me in the summer of 1959 that he was still determined to prove me and the Fisheries officer wrong by spending the early part of the following October on the upper Babine. This he did, and subsequently wrote me the following account of his experiences:

"As for Norlakes Lodge I was there during the first eleven days of October. I caught one twelve pound steelhead on my first day. Then followed a week during which I caught nothing but a few cohoe and a number of Dolly Varden. During the last three days of my visit, however, I landed six steelhead running from eight to eleven pounds. A few steelhead were caught in September but I feel the run wasn't really under way when I left. Weather on the Babine was abominable."

In October of 1960, Bill Fife made his most recent visit to the upper Babine. After his return to the States he reported to me that he had had even better steelhead fishing than he had experienced in the fall of 1959. He also told me of a party of four that had fished the upper Babine during the second week of October 1960 and reported landing over 200 steelhead during this period. With this wealth of evidence available, I am ready to agree that the Babine must be a magnificent steelhead river, if fished at the right time of the year.

Another surprising piece of information about the Babine came to me recently from Buzz Fiorini. In response to my inquiry, Buzz stated that the finest rainbow trout fishing he had ever experienced in his life was on the upper Babine in early July. The chief reason for my surprise was the belief that at this time of the year all streams in the Skeena Valley are flooded by the heavy run-off of snow from the mountains. Buzz then told me that, because there are no mountain ranges of any consequence close to Babine Lake, the river remains relatively low during the early summer months. Buzz Fiorini has never fished the Morice so we had no basis for a direct comparison of this stream with the Babine. Nevertheless, he has been on so many other fine streams in his fishing career that I can only accept his evidence as conclusive proof that the Babine must be rated with the finest rainbow trout rivers in the whole area.

IV *The Kispiox*

THE KISPIOX RIVER is probably the most famous steelhead stream in the world today, and for a fly fisherman is also the most frustrating I have ever known. When the water is relatively low and clear the Kispiox is a beautiful stream to fish. It is easy to wade, has many lovely pools and long stretches of swift water.

The trouble is that I have rarely found it in this condition. As mentioned in the preceding chapter, the Kispiox does not have for its source a large lake which always has an important stabilizing influence on the condition of the water in the stream below it. Instead, the Kispiox originates in numerous small mountain streams, and, as a result, rises rapidly and becomes discolored after even one day of heavy rain.

My introduction to this river occurred in a somewhat unusual manner. When I flew out of Morice Lake with Hal Hentz and Hunter Perry at the end of the first week of September 1954, I stayed on for one more week to fish the lower streams. The first three days were spent fishing the lower Morice in the company of Hentz and Perry. My friends then departed for the United States, and I moved on downstream to the Bulkley River. For the next three days I fished alone at various spots on the Bulkley without any tangible results.

The evening of the sixth day found me stopping in a little hotel at Smithers. There I met a local taxi driver named Buck Morris who subsequently served me as a guide and also as a fine fishing companion. Buck told me that if I really wanted steelhead he would take me to the Kispiox River about sixty miles farther downstream. At that time I had never heard of the Kispiox, and I am sure it was virtually unknown outside of the immediate vicinity. With only one more day of fishing left I was delighted and accepted eagerly. We left before dawn the next day and reached the junction of the Kispiox and the Skeena about nine in the morning.

At that time the motor road along the bank of the river could be negotiated by automobiles for about fifteen miles upstream from the mouth of the Kispiox. This road, incidentally, had been constructed around the turn of the century as part of the old Telegraph Trail which carried the first telegraph line up into the Yukon Territory. After following the Kispiox for about twenty miles this old trail cut across country to the Skeena River and then ran along the banks of the latter stream to the north.

Starting at the mouth of the river we worked our way slowly upstream, fishing each attractive pool that we saw. The water was low and clear, and a joy to fish. Late in the afternoon we reached a point about 12 miles up from the mouth and there ran into the only other fisherman that we saw all day on the river. When we met him, this man had just landed a 15 pound steelhead on spinning tackle.

During the course of the day, Buck Morris, using a big spinning rod and large Tee-spoons, captured three steelhead which weighed 14, 12 and 8 pounds respectively. My score was about a dozen small rainbow and Dolly Varden trout, but I had not a single steeelhead strike. I used an assortment of both wet and dry flies. My wet flies were not the best varieties for steelhead, and I had yet to learn that my dry flies would not work on steelhead under any and all conditions. Nevertheless, I was greatly intrigued by the beauty of the stream and its potentialities for steelhead, and I made up my mind to return the following year.

This I did, in the company of Smith Richardson, and again escorted by Buck Morris. When our party flew out of Morice Lake on September 17, 1955, Smith and I stayed on at Hazelton for the balance of the month. Of this period we fished eight days on the Kispiox, two on the lower Babine as already recounted in the preceding chapter, and the other three days on some minor streams and lakes in the vicinity.

Unfortunately, the water in the Kispiox was high and fairly muddy from the almost continuous heavy rains during the latter half of September. In addition, we found the stream literally crawling with spin fishermen from all over North America. Most of them had been attracted to the river by an article in the June issue of "Field and Stream". This article had reported the taking of two world record steelhead from the Kispiox in the fall of 1954, one weighing 36 pounds and the second 33 pounds. In all, according to the article, six of the ten largest steelhead caught anywhere in 1954 and recorded, had come out of the Kispiox.

These spin fishermen were using hardware of every kind, but there was one particularly murderous type of equipment in widespread use. It consisted of a large spinning rod with 20 pound test monofilament line. At the end of the line was attached a cheesecloth bag filled with salmon eggs and a bunch of gang hooks. About four feet above the hooks was a lead weight about the size and shape of an ordinary pencil. This heavy weight was attached to the line by means of an elastic rubber tube, the spring in the rubber tending to prevent the weight from snagging on the bottom. The fishermen would cast this strange paraphernalia upstream and let it come bouncing down over the rocks. With the bag of salmon eggs drifting along close to the bottom of the stream, it was almost certain to take any steelhead in the vicinity.

It is pleasant to report that since 1956 the British Columbia Department of Fisheries has prohibited the use of salmon eggs by fishermen on the Skeena River and on all of its tributaries. This is an important step in the right direction but unfortunately there are certain other types of hardware that are almost as deadly as salmon eggs for steelhead. In particular, the very popular Tee-spoon deserves mention. If I were a meat fisherman I would use nothing but these big lures and would almost guarantee to take my full share of steelhead in any river. It has a large silver spoon which spins around a row of red plastic nodules that look like the heads of golf tees to a fisherman, and like salmon eggs to the trout.

While we were on the Kispiox, the spin fishermen were having a field day, while the few stubborn addicts of the flyrod, like myself, had very lean pickings. In eight days of fishing I landed just one steelhead of 15 pounds and lost two others. Among the three other fly fishermen whom I encountered, I learned of only one other steelhead landed on a fly.

Meanwhile in one day I saw Buck Morris land six fine steelhead out of a single pool with his large Tee-spoons. I saw one steelhead landed weighing 32 pounds and several others over 20 pounds. Although we did not see the fish, we were told that the Indians had netted a 41 pounder near their village at the mouth of the river.

The "Field and Stream" statistics for 1955 showed for the Kispiox an even more amazing record than that of 1954. According to these figures, the six largest steelhead landed anywhere in 1955 on spinning tackle were taken from the Kispiox. These fish ran from just under 33 pounds to just over 26 pounds. Moreover, the three largest steelhead taken on flies also came from the Kispiox and ran from 29 pounds to just under 26 pounds. Incidentally, my unreported 15 pounder was exactly the same weight as the tenth largest steelhead reported taken anywhere on a fly in 1955. No mention is made in these statistics of the use of salmon eggs but from what I saw on the stream in 1955, I would make a fairly substantial wager that at least some of these big fish were taken in this manner.

My solitary steelhead was a dark male which was obviously a sexually mature fish. I hooked it at the upper end of a deep pool where an eddy in the current sucked my white Maribou streamer down to the bottom. When the fish struck I was sure I was snagged. It then fought sullenly and stubbornly and never once leaped clear of the water. Because of this, and the darkness of the fish, I became resigned to the belief that I had hooked a large cohoe salmon.

I worked my way slowly down stream, keeping the fish above me and thus making it fight the current as well as my line. My only tough problem was getting past a large fallen tree which extended far out into the river. I finally managed to negotiate this obstacle, but not without feeling some very cold water slop in over the top of my chest waders. The fish was eventually beached at the edge of a large pool several hundred yards below the point where I hooked it. It was only then that I realized I had landed a large steelhead.

Our visit to the Kispiox in 1955 could not be called a success by any measure. The only benefit for me was the gaining of some additional

Hunter Perry playing rainbow trout from bow of boat on Upper Morice

Author casting on wide stretch of Upper Morice River

The fish counting weir at the head of the Babine River

Babine River looking downstream from fish weir

knowledge of the habits of steelhead. Thus, I soon learned that this was not a river suitable for the use of dry flies. If one was to have any hope of hooking steelhead on a fly, it could only be accomplished with a deeply sunken wet fly worked slowly through the water where these fish might be likely to be found. A sinking line was important and weighted flies were usually the best bet. I saw for the first time the use of weighted lines by two fly fishermen from California. I would never use such tackle because of the great strain it must put on a rod. Besides, it seems unnecessary for anyone who knows the elementary principle of sinking a fly by casting at an upstream angle and then permitting the fly to drift unhindered downstream for some distance.

Most of the wet flies I saw were the standard types commonly used on the steelhead streams in Oregon and Washington. For myself, I depended mainly on the optic flies which had proved successful on the lower Morice. My single steelhead, however, was taken on a white maribou streamer, which is certainly not a typical steelhead fly. While on the river we met Jack Horner, a professional fly-tier from San Francisco, who introduced us to the Horner shrimp flies. These were weighted deer hair streamers, bright red or orange in color, with two tiny silver beads placed at the head of the fly to represent the bulging eyes of a shrimp. I have since used them with considerable success on other streams.

I must be more than usually stubborn or dumb. Almost anyone else, I am sure, would have been happy to look for greener pastures than the Kispiox, after the experiences I had in 1954 and 1955. Instead, I was destined to come back for one more try at this river in the fall of 1959.

My undoing in this regard came about as a result of an accidental meeting with a young farmer who lived close to the river. This young Scottish-Canadian named Dundas, had fiery red hair and brilliant pink cheeks. He told us enthusiastically of huge rainbow trout, of six and eight pounds, that could be caught about 25 miles upstream from the end of the motor road, and near the junction of Sweetin Creek and the Kispiox. He advised us that he was prepared to provide pack horses for such a trip, and assured us of magnificent hunting as well as fishing.

My imagination was fired by the story, but I was unable to arrange a trip to the upper Kispiox until the fall of 1959. When I started working on plans for this trip as early as November of 1958 I ran immediately into the usual impenetrable fog of the lack of local information. Not knowing how to locate Dundas by letter, I employed my friend Buck Morris of Smithers to make a special trip to the Kispiox to locate the young man. Buck reported back that he found the Dundas family had moved away to parts unknown. He then suggested I write for information to Vic Giraud, a fisheries officer located in the town of Terrace. This I did, and in due course was advised that I should get in touch with Jack Lee of Hazleton, a licensed guide who was prepared to take pack trips up the Kispiox.

Some months later I established contact with Jack Lee and arrangements were made for a pack trip with a party of four during the first two weeks of September. When I passed this information on to Buck Morris I received the unexpected reply that he had known the Lees for years; that Jack was the finest guide, and his wife, Frances, the finest camp cook in the whole valley. Buck then went on to explain that it just had not occurred to him that Lee was still in the guiding business.

Further surprises were in store for us. Jack's laconic letters merely advised that he would provide horses, guides, and all the equipment necessary for a pack trip as far up the Kispiox as we cared to go. He wrote that the first two weeks of September would be ideal for grizzly bear hunting because salmon would be spawning in the river at the time. We would be somewhat too early for the best moose shooting but mountain goat would be available on the nearby ranges. He added finally that we should find excellent fishing near the mouth of Sweetin Creek.

Our party consisted of Charlie Calderini and Tom Cassady from Chicago, Bob Fisher from Keokuk, Iowa, and myself. We flew from Chicago to Smithers in Fisher's Aero Commander plane, arriving at noon on Sunday, August 30. We had arranged for Buck Morris to take us the following morning to the head of the motor road on the Kispiox where, as we supposed, we were to be met by Jack Lee and the pack train. It was not until we were already several miles up the river that I learned that the motor road during the preceding year had been extended for another 25 miles upstream and now terminated at the mouth of Sweetin Creek.

When we met Jack Lee and his brother-in-law, Wally Love, they were accompanied by two Jeep trucks instead of the train of pack horses which we had expected. We were then driven in these Jeeps for a final ten miles over a section of the new road which was practically impassable for ordinary cars. Here, without previous warning, we arrived at Corral Creek Camp, which we discovered was Jack Lee's hunting and fishing lodge.

The camp consisted of a brand new and commodious main cabin where Mrs. Lee presided as cook, and two small adjoining cabins that furnished sleeping quarters for two guests each. The whole set-up was located on a high and beautiful promontory overlooking the Kispiox about five miles below the new terminus of the road.

We found Jack Lee all prepared with horses, guides, and equipment to set out the next day with us on a pack trip. He told us, however, that the fishing and hunting in the vicinity of the lodge were as good as anything we could find further upstream. After realizing the comfort of our quarters and sampling Frances Lee's delicious cooking, we all decided to remain at Corral Creek Camp for the entire two weeks. It is fortunate that we made this decision, because during our visit, we had only one really clear day.

The result, of course, of the almost continuous rains was that the Kispiox was high and discolored throughout our stay. Except for the cohoe salmon which we all caught in considerable numbers, the fishing on the river was almost wholly barren of results. The only sample of the huge rainbows promised by young Dundas was one four-pounder that Charlie Calderini took on spinning tackle. We also took a fair number of Dolly Varden trout but, as previously reported, we regarded these as a nuisance rather than as good sport.

We saw no steelhead in the river, and I had only one heavy strike that might have been a steelhead. I did land two ten-inch rainbows which were probably young steelhead taken prior to their migration to salt water. While I realized we were on the river somewhat too early for the heavy fall run, there was good reason to hope that enough steelhead would be in the Kispiox to provide good fishing. There were certainly plenty of these fish in the river when I first visited it on September 12, 1954. On our 1959 trip, however, we received occasional reports from downstream which informed us that only a very few steelhead had been seen or caught in the lower sections of the river.

The cohoe salmon fishing, particularly near the mouth of Sweetin Creek, provided surprisingly good sport. Most of these fish were fairly bright in color, and several that I hooked on wet flies ran and jumped like steelhead. The flesh of the bright cohoes was firm and furnished delicious eating.

For Charlie Calderini and Bob Fisher the lack of steelhead was a matter of minor importance. These two were not much interested in fly fishing and had come on the trip primarily to shoot grizzly bear and moose. Since they found good hunting, as will be reported in a subsequent chapter, Charlie and Bob were perfectly happy. My chief concern was with Tom Cassady, who had no interest in hunting, and came only for the fishing. For myself, the absence of steelhead was a disappointment but not too important because I knew I would find good steelhead fishing later in the month on the Sustut and Johanson Rivers.

One saving grace for Cassady and me was the excellent rainbow fishing we found in two small lakes near the camp. We fished these lakes from rubber rafts which Jack Lee owned. The lake rainbows rose eagerly to dry flies and provided almost continuous activity. Most of them were between 10 and 14 inches in length, although Tom landed several of over two pounds.

We also discovered that the ideal way to fish a stream like the Kispiox is with the use of a rubber raft. On several occasions Tom and I floated several miles downstream in one of these rafts. In this manner we were able to fish many beautiful pools which we could never have reached on foot. We would put the raft into the river at some spot and make arrangements with a guide to meet us with the Jeep truck at a predetermined point some miles further downstream. It was very pleasant to drift silently down the river in a rubber raft, slowly at times and then swiftly through the many stretches of rapids. The snow-capped coastal range provided a magnificent scenic backdrop for these trips, and almost every turn in the river gave us a slightly different view of these beautiful peaks. With two men on board, one handling a small pair of oars, and the other using a paddle to steer, these rafts were easy to maneuver and seemed fairly safe.

During our entire visit we encountered only one lone fisherman on the Upper Kispiox. This man was as weird a character as I have ever met. One day while motoring down the road in one of the Jeep trucks a few miles below our camp we met this individual walking by himself in the opposite direction. We learned that he was headed for the mouth of Sweetin Creek and had just been deposited on the road by a taxicab from Hazelton at a point beyond which ordinary cars dared not go. He carried a spinning rod and had a small knapsack on his back. From the size of his pack we could see that it was clearly too small to contain a sleeping bag. Our guess was that all he had was a small coffee pot, a frying pan, some coffee and a few extra articles of clothing.

The next time we saw this man was three days later when our guide, Wally Love, and I went up to Sweetin Creek to spend the afternoon fishing. There we found him attempting to cast into a big pool at the junction of the two streams. From his fumbling maneuvers it was apparent that he knew nothing about handling a spinning rod. As soon as we started to fish he stood aside to watch, and admitted he had yet to catch his first fish.

I suddenly realized that the poor devil must be on the point of starvation and decided to give him any fish that we might catch. Although his speech had become almost incoherent he managed to tell us that he was an office worker in the British Columbia Forestry Department at Vancouver. He had read about the Kispiox River and had decided to spend a week of his vacation on the stream. It is hard to imagine how anyone could be so insane as to wander off into the wilderness by himself, without food, without a gun, without any protection against the cold, and armed only with a fishing rod which he had no idea how to use.

Within a short time Wally had landed a bright 14 pound cohoe on spinning tackle and soon thereafter I took a 12 pounder on a wet fly. When I handed these fish to our friend, he grabbed them without a word and bolted off into the brush in the direction of a small abandoned cabin where apparently he had been staying. We soon saw a column of smoke rising from the chimney and judged that Robinson Crusoe was about to enjoy his first meal in three days. He never reappeared that afternoon, and we did not see him again. We could only guess that somehow Divine Providence had enabled him to find his way back to civilization. The experience strengthened my conviction that there is no possible way of saving a fool from his folly.

I left the Kispiox on September 11 to join three Canadian friends at the town of Terrace for a trip to Sustut Lake. The other three members of our Kispiox party stayed on at Jack Lee's camp for two more days, and were then driven back to Smithers by Buck Morris. From there they flew back to the United States in Bob Fisher's plane.

A few general comments about fishing the Kispiox are now in order. First, there can be no doubt that the story by young Dundas of huge rainbows in the Upper Kispiox was a great exaggeration, even if it was not manufactured out of whole cloth. If such fish had been there in any numbers we certainly would have taken more than Charlie Calderini's lone four-pounder. As a matter of fact, if I had considered the matter properly in advance, I should not have been as fooled as I was. Thus, it has been my experience in fishing these rivers of the far north that the only spots where I have found resident trout in large quantities are just below the outlets of large lakes.

It seems to me more than a mere coincidence that streams such as the upper Morice and upper Babine provide the only first-rate rainbow fishing that I have seen in this area. I am convinced that the lakes out of which these rivers flow provide excellent winter homes for the trout. As a result, the fish, particularly the small fry, find protection from the destructive effects of the break-up of the ice in the spring and the heavy flooding of the rivers. If this theory is correct, one would expect to find, as in fact I have, relatively few resident trout in streams, such as the Kispiox, the lower Morice, and the lower Babine.

It is also probably true that trout survive the rigorous winters in this area much better in large deep lakes like Morice and Babine than they do in smaller bodies of water. The reason, I am sure, is that the supply of oxygen in a heavily frozen small lake is likely to be insufficient to permit the survival of fish. Thus, I have found no rainbows near the outlets of Sustut Lake or of Johanson Lake. Both are much smaller in size than either Babine Lake or Morice Lake, and since both are much higher above sea level the thickness of the winter ice is certain to be much greater.

If the Good Lord could guarantee me low, clear water for a week or ten days around the end of September or early in October, I should love to return to the Kispiox. I would stay at Jack Lee's attractive lodge and fish the upper river for steelhead with a rubber raft. Although doubtless I would take fewer fish than the wielder of a spinning rod, I am confident that I would land enough steelhead on a fly to make me happy.

The weather being such as I have found it, the Kispiox is clearly a river for the spinning rod enthusiast rather than for an addict of the fly rod such as myself. Buck Morris certainly had a point when he confided one day to Buzz Fiorini that "Mr. Fennelly is a very nice man, but he must be nuts to go on using a fly rod when he could have so much more fun and catch so many more steelhead using a spinning rod."

I must plead guilty to the charge. My trouble is that I greatly enjoy every aspect of fly fishing but find no pleasure in heaving out a big spoon with a spinning rod. The result is that I am happier with a small number of fish taken with flies than I would be with a much larger number caught with spinning tackle. It may be a matter of purely personal prejudice, but I am sure that I am now too old to attempt a change in my habits.

From the comments made above about the bad weather on the Kispiox one might easily get the impression that the weather is uniformly bad in the Skeena Valley in the fall. Such has not been my experience. In 1951, 1953, 1954, and the first half of September 1955, we had almost nothing but fine, clear days. It was only during the latter half of September 1955, and all of September 1959, that we ran into continuous rains. I am afraid it is true that the later in the fall one stays in the Skeena Valley the more one is likely to encounter rain and cold. If you are a fly fisherman and wish to cope with the big fall runs of steelhead you should confine your efforts to rivers like the Morice, the Babine, and the Sustut which remain clear and fishable despite heavy fall rains.

A few brief comments must be made about the extraordinary size of the steelhead that have been taken on the Kispiox. The largest fish I have heard of taken on the Morice was 18 pounds, and I understand that a few steelhead over 20 pounds have been caught on the Sustut and Johanson Rivers. Nevertheless, I am sure that the average size of these fish and of those taken on other tributaries of the Skeena are smaller than most of the steelhead caught on the Kispiox. The Kispiox steelhead are generally thicker through the body and almost look like a different breed from the streamlined, torpedo-like bodies of the steelhead in other tributaries.

The only answer I can give for this phenomenon is the influence of heredity. As mentioned previously, each stream seems to have its own separate run of steelhead, and the time of each run bears little relationship to that of the runs on other rivers in the Skeena watershed. What this means, as I see it, is a return to the river of its birth by every steelhead that comes in from the ocean. For some unknown reasons the ancestors of the Kispiox steelhead were bigger and thicker than those that originated in other tributaries, and the present descendants of these fish show the same inherited characteristics.

Another peculiarity of the Kispiox steelhead is the sexual maturity of the fall run of fish in this river. Practically all of the steelhead I have seen taken from the Kispiox have been much darker in color and in a more advanced state of sexual development than those seen at the same time of the year on other Skeena tributaries. A recent bulletin by the Chief Fisheries Biologist of the British Columbia Game Commission calls attention to this fact. In describing the characteristics of summer and fall-run steelhead, it states, "There appear to be exceptions to the above since the Kispiox run seems to be composed of sexually mature fish arriving there in a mature condition in the fall."

The result is that the Kispiox steelhead must be angled for by methods suitable for typical winter-run fish. They either lie at the bottom of deep pools or else move swiftly upstream toward their spawning grounds. They cannot be induced to rise to dry flies and can only be hooked by a deeply sunken wet fly or by some form of brightly flashing spoon.

With a motor road now running about 40 miles along the banks of the river, and with hundreds of fishermen throwing hardware into the

water every fall, it seems inevitable that the steelhead fishing in the
Kispiox will gradually deteriorate. It is much more difficult, of course,
to destroy runs of migratory fish than it is to wipe out the resident
trout in a river. Nevertheless, I am sure the same thing will happen
to the Kispiox that has occurred on many steelhead streams in the
United States. The average size of the steelhead, as well as the number
of fish taken, will gradually fall off. For many years, however, the
Kispiox should continue to be a magnificent steelhead stream for those
who fish it with equipment suitable for the condition of the water
at the time.

V *The Sustut and The Johanson*

M Y FIRST CAST on the upper Sustut River was with a dry fly. The big Grizzly Wulff bounced lightly down the riffle and was hit by a large splashing rise near the lower end of the pool. I was fast to a good steelhead which jumped twice and then ran out into a wide shallow bay. When it finally came into the beach about 40 minutes later I found I had an unusually bright fish weighing just over 12 pounds. While I was playing this fish, two other members of our party hooked steelhead in the same pool. Thus, we found ourselves with three wildly charging fish on at the same time. Somehow we managed to keep our lines from being tangled, and all three were landed. When we finished our first evening of fishing on the Sustut, our four rods had taken five good steelhead.

We had flown that same afternoon, September 12, 1959, from the town of Terrace in a chartered plane. In our party were Brian Magee, Gus Craig, and Ron Sanderson, all from Toronto, and myself. When we put down on the Sustut Lake about 4:00 p.m., we were met by Buzz Fiorini, professional "white hunter" and trip manager. Also waiting us were Hunter Simpson, white guide and cook, and two Indian guides, David Bob and Dominic Abrahams. The Indians had already set up for us one tent camp at the lower end of Sustut Lake, and another some six miles downstream where the Sustut is joined by Johanson Creek.

As shown by the map on the inside cover, Sustut Lake and Johanson Lake are located in the northeastern corner of the Skeena watershed.

These two small lakes lie in rugged mountain country and are about 25 miles apart. Both are narrow bodies of water, Sustut being about six miles long, and Johanson about four. Sustut Lake is divided into two parts: the main body of water, and a lower shallow bay about a half mile in diameter. Connecting the two is a slowly flowing stream about half a mile in length. This little stretch of the upper Sustut River was packed with steelhead during our entire stay in the area, with fresh fish coming into the lower pools almost daily to replace those that moved on up into the main body of Sustut Lake.

Although I first heard of the Sustut and Johanson Rivers in 1955, I had to wait four years for my first visit. The original information came from the fisheries officer who visited our camp on Morice Lake in the fall of 1955. In addition to telling us that the Babine was a very poor steelhead stream, he informed us that the Sustut and Johanson were the finest steelhead rivers in the entire Skeena watershed.

Then and there I determined to visit these rivers, and shortly after my return to the States in 1955 began making inquiries as to how to arrange a trip to this remote wilderness area. There are no motor roads within 125 miles of Sustut Lake, and the nearest human settlements are the Indian villages of Babine and Takla Landing, each more than 100 miles to the south. I realized there would be no difficulty in chartering a plane to fly into Sustut Lake, but arranging for supplies, equipment and guides once you arrived was very different.

I soon discovered that a man named Mac Anderson had built a hunting and fishing lodge on Bear Lake about 60 miles south of Sustut, and was prepared to fly parties from there into Sustut and Johanson Lakes. Before I was able to get in touch with Anderson, however, I learned that he had been drowned on the Bear River, and no information was forthcoming as to what had happened to his lodge.

Believing that this country was almost a Terra Incognita, and that I held a secret known to few outsiders, I was astonished to see the whole story laid out on the back cover of the 1957 Orvis Christmas catalogue. In addition to a picture of Johanson Lake, there was one of Buzz Fiorini displaying three huge steelhead. These three fish, weighing a total of just under 60 pounds, were taken by Fiorini in one afternoon in a pool just below the outlet of the main body of Sustut Lake.

Correspondence with Fiorini quickly brought forth the information that Driftwood Lodge on Bear Lake was now owned by a Mr. Acker of Los Angeles. I passed this story on to my friend, Gus Craig of Toronto, who started at once to make arrangements for a trip in the fall of 1958. I was unable to join him because Mrs. Fennelly and I had already made plans to spend our 1958 vacation fishing for Atlantic salmon in New Brunswick and Nova Scotia.

Gus Craig brought back from his trip enthusiastic reports of the finest steelhead fishing he had ever experienced. It was inevitable, therefore, that a visit to this country in the following fall should be organized. Although Driftwood Lodge was not opened for commercial use in 1959, we were able to make arrangements with the owners for the use of their tents, boats and the log cabin on Johanson Lake. Buzz Fiorini, using his own float plane, flew in the guides and all necessary supplies and met us on our arrival at Sustut Lake.

We spent our first night in the tent camp on Sustut Lake, and the following morning the whole party trekked the six miles downstream to our second camp at the junction of the Sustut with Johanson Creek. At least half of the so-called trail was over muskeg, and provided my first experience with this abominable stuff. Continuous rains had turned the ground into a quagmire, and on each step through the high grass you never knew whether your foot would rest on a firm hummock or whether you would sink in water halfway to your knees. All of us were wearing high hunting boots which were supposed to be water-proof, but none arrived at the junction without soaking feet. Under the circumstances, I envied the Indians their light moccasins which became no more filled with water than our expensive boots.

The terrain drops sharply about a mile below the lower bay of Sustut Lake. As a result, the stream is an almost continuous cascade with no good holding water for steelhead until the river reaches a spot within a couple of hundred yards of the junction. From here on the country begins to flatten out, and the river, while still fast flowing, has a series of beautiful pools beginning at the junction and continuing down-stream for more than a mile.

Crossing the Sustut about a half mile above the junction was an exciting incident. At this point the stream was a narrow torrent of white water, obviously impossible to wade. A tree about six inches in diameter had been felled across the river to serve as a bridge. I watched two of my companions walk this tight rope without difficulty, and I knew that I had to make the attempt. After three or four uncertain steps out over the water, I began to wobble and realized I would never get across. Just then I felt the strong hands of Dominic, one of our Indian guides, supporting me from the rear. With his sure-footed assistance I made the other bank without further trouble.

When we reached our camp we found the big pool at the junction full of steeelhead. This pool, deep and swift at the upper end where the two streams meet, is about 100 feet long and fairly narrow. The clear gravel bottom slopes gradually upward toward the tail where the water is only about two feet deep. The slower water of the lower part of the pool formed a perfect holding spot for steelhead, and we usually could see at least a dozen lying there in three to four feet of water.

That first afternoon we all fished this big pool and each of us landed several good steelhead. My three, weighing 10, 12 and 14 pounds, were all taken on wet flies. The chief difficulty in fishing this water was caused by a large island just below the pool which divided the river into two separate channels. The larger flow of water swept down the right side of the island and contained relatively few snags. The channel on the left side of the island, however, was narrower and full of snags and fallen trees. If your fish started on a downstream rush you always had a few bad moments while attempting to maneuver it into the larger channel. Although I did succeed in landing one steelhead in the left-hand channel, a considerable number of others were lost by our party to snags in this section of the stream.

The 14 pounder that I hooked the first afternoon made three jumps and then started headlong downstream. I barely managed to steer it into the right hand channel and scrambled madly in pursuit. When the big steelhead was checked briefly in a small pool about half-way down the island, I succeeded in getting below it and thought I was beginning to assert some control over the fish. Very soon, however, my fish started downstream again and continued going right on through two more small pools. When I finally beached the steelhead, I found myself in a large pool some distance below the lower end of the island.

That night it rained heavily and the next morning we found the river several inches higher but still clear. Gus Craig, Brian Magee, and Buzz Fiorini took off downstream to explore some of the lower pools while Ron Sanderson and I stayed at camp to fish the Junction Pool. Around 10:00 a.m., I hooked and landed a 10 pounder on a dry fly. About an hour later both Ron and I had almost simultaneous heavy strikes. I was using a Skykomish wet fly while Ron had a tiny Gibb Stewart spoon attached to his leader. My fish, a bright 15 pound steelhead, carried me several hundred yards down the right side of the island and took me more than 45 minutes to land.

When I came back to the Junction Pool I found Ron still battling his fish. I shouted at him that, since the sun was practically over the yardarm, I was going into camp for a drink. After pulling off my waders, I poured out two drinks of Scotch whiskey and returned to the edge of the stream to watch the battle. Time and again Ron would work his big fish into the shore only to see it slip out once more into the current. Almost another hour elapsed before he finally beached the steelhead. By that time I had consumed his drink as well as my own. When he brought the fish into camp it registered just over 19 pounds on my de-liar. This proved to be the largest steelhead taken by any of us on the trip.

The second night it rained again and the next morning we found the river at least a foot higher than it had been on our arrival. The water was beginning to get dirty and the current had become dangerously heavy for wading. Nevertheless, each of us managed to land one or more steelhead during the day. The one nine pounder that I landed provided much less excitement than the two fish that I lost.

The first loss occurred in the morning while Gus Craig and I were fishing the Junction Pool. He was casting from the small bar on the right side of the stream while I was working from the left bank. Gus had a heavy strike in the middle of the pool and his fish started downstream. Believing that I would not interfere, I continued casting into the deep water at the upper end of the pool. Because of the heavy current and discolored water I was using a wet fly with a small golden spinner just above it.

Very soon I had a good strike and immediately entered the water near the lower end of the pool in an effort to keep my fish above me. Almost simultaneously Craig's fish started upstream and mine started downstream. Our lines crossed and I found myself floundering and struggling to keep my balance in a very heavy current almost waist deep. Gus, who is a powerfully built man over six feet in height, worked his way over to my side, passed his line over mine, and we were both free.

My fish then turned and ran upstream through the head of the pool and on into Johanson Creek. While the steelhead was still moving against the current my line suddenly went slack on a straight pull-out of the small fly. I reeled in and walked up the bank to watch Craig's continuing battle. His steelhead had turned to the right at the head of the pool and had continued far up into the long quiet pool of the Sustut above the junction.

All members of our party now gathered to watch, and it was Buzz Fiorini who first noticed that the big fish had been foul-hooked just above the tail. At his request one of our Indians brought a large landing net from camp. The fish now seemed pretty well spent and was lying quietly with head downstream in about four feet of water. Buzz and I entered the river and attempted to lower the net in front of the fish. The latter, however, made one final effort, broke free and was gone. This steelhead was unusually large and must have weighed at least 18 pounds.

The second incident took place in the afternoon when Buzz and I were fishing together in a pool about a half mile below the junction. Here the river took a right angle turn of almost 90 degrees. Just below the turn, and jutting out into the stream from the left bank was a large boulder. The quiet water below this rock was an excellent holding spot for steelhead and we usually found several lying there.

I soon spotted a large fish in about four feet of water and began drifting a dry fly over it. After about 15 minutes of casting without any reaction from the steelhead I shifted to a Skykomish wet fly. On the third or fourth cast the fish struck and started tearing off line in a downstream run. Unfortunately, the water under the relatively high bank was too deep to wade, and for more than one hundred yards below me a great many alder bushes extended well out over the stream.

Buzz saw my predicament and volunteered to help. Time and again we passed the rod from one to the other in getting the line around these obstacles. We finally succeeded in working past the last of the bushes and reached wadeable water.

I now found myself at the head of a long curving pool with a wide gravel beach on my side of the river and a high cut bank on the far side. In this water I was sure I could bring the fish under control. Several times I worked it into the shore only to see it wriggle off again into the current. At the lower end of the pool there was a heavy rapids with an impassable bank on my side of the stream. When my fish was about 20 feet above the rapids I made one last desperate effort to bring it ashore, and the leader parted. This, incidentally, was the only time I lost a fly to a steelhead during our entire visit.

A third successive night of rain made us realize on Wednesday morning that it would be a waste of time to stay on any longer at the junction. The river was over its banks at our campsite and the bar on the opposite side of the Junction Pool had disappeared. We decided, therefore, to hike back to Sustut Lake where we knew that the little stretch of stream below the outlet of the main body of the lake would be unaffected by the rains.

For three successive days we had excellent steelhead fishing at Sustut Lake. The last two of these days were bright and sunny. The clouds lifted from the mountains and, for the first time, we had an opportunity to appreciate the beauty of the scene. All along the southwest shore of Sustut Lake and for many miles below it ran a high range of snow capped mountains. The highest point in this range was Sustut Peak with an elevation of 8,100 feet. On the northeast shore was another lower range of mountains, rising to about 6,500 feet. This northern range was bare of snow, except for a few isolated patches.

The shores of the lake were heavily wooded, the forest rising up along the mountain sides for about 600 feet before it disappeared at the timber line. Above this there was nothing but brown grass, bare rock, and snow. It was late fall at Sustut Lake, and, except for the eternal green of the pines, all the colors were soft pastel shades of yellow and brown. Moose were frequent visitors to the shores of the lake, and black duck flew back and forth all day long between the lower bay

Author weighing 17-pound steelhead taken on the Sustut

Ron Sanderson with 19-pound steelhead taken at Junction Pool

and the upper lake. Occasionally we would hear the lonesome cry of a loon, and on clear nights the sound of wolves was all around us.

Although we all caught a considerable number of steelhead, five rods in action made the fishing on the short stretch of water somewhat unsatisfactory. Most of the steelhead were congregated in two large pools. The first fisherman who cast into one of these schools almost invariably hooked a steelhead. Then immediately all the rest of the fish would scatter and an hour or more would elapse before they would school up again. In the slow clear water these steelhead were the spookiest fish I have ever seen.

On Saturday Buzz Fiorini ferried the whole party to Johanson Lake in his float plane. Because of the altitude of the lake, and the small capacity of his little Cessna 180, he had to make four separate trips.

When we arrived at Johanson we found ourselves above the timber line. Except for a scattering of small bushes, the whole shoreline was covered with brown and yellow grass, with the bare rocks of the mountains rising steeply on three sides of the lake. Like Sustut, Johanson Lake is divided into a main body of water and a lower shallow bay. Connecting the two is a short channel of about two hundred yards and containing only one good riffle.

The lower bay is surrounded by low, bare hills, and Johanson Creek breaks out through a narrow gap about half way down the right side of the bay. The stream then cascades straight downhill for a drop of two to three hundred feet before being checked at the first large pool. The scene reminded me of an elongated soup tureen with a deep crack on on side. From the crest of the low hills we could always see large numbers of steelhead cruising around the bay, looking black under the water when viewed from above.

The fishing at Johanson proved disappointing. On each of three successive days my first or second cast into the riffle at the head of the bay produced a good steelhead. Immediately thereafter all the other fish in or near the riffle scattered, and no one caught any more fish there for the rest of the day. In the still water of the bay, each of these fish required an incredible length of time to land with my 5¼-ounce fly rod, and one 13 pounder took almost all of my 200 yards of backing.

Although I spent many hours casting for the cruising fish in the bay I never succeeded in getting one to strike my wet flies. On the other hand, Brian Magee landed several from the bay with the use of a spinning rod and a large Tee-spoon. We spent one day fishing several of the lower pools of Johanson Creek, but Ron Sanderson was the only one of our party who took a steelhead from the stream itself. This fish he spotted resting behind a rock halfway down the steep cascade leading out of the bay. He cast to it with a spoon, hooked the fish, and finally landed it in the big pool below.

For the three nights at Johanson we slept in the comparative luxury of a small log cabin that belonged to the owners of Driftwood Lodge. This was the only occasion on which we had any heat in our sleeping quarters during our fifteen day visit to this area. It was fortunate that we had a warm cabin because at almost 5,000 feet the nights at Johanson Lake were very cold.

One disappointment to me was the almost complete absence of snow on the surrounding mountains. This was surprising because earlier in the month the lower mountains around the Kispiox had been heavily covered with snow. When Gus Craig was at Johanson in late September of 1958 a snowfall of several inches had covered the whole area. Gus told us that, in this setting, Johanson Lake was the most beautiful body of water he had ever seen.

After three bright days the weather turned bad again. Fearing that we might be isolated at Johanson Lake we decided to make a quick exit back to Sustut Lake. Brian Magee and I were the last two to be ferried out by Fiorini. The ceiling was dropping fast and Buzz just barely managed to get into Sustut under the clouds.

We found that during our absence our camp had been raided by a grizzly bear. He had torn our tent to shreds and chewed up all our luggage, scattering the contents all over the landscape. My pigskin bag was destroyed beyond repair. I have preserved as a souvenir, however, a small leather manicure set with bear tooth marks all through it. Although Hunter Simpson did a fine job of repair with a large needle and string, only a small area of the tent proved to be waterproof during the subsequent nights of almost continuous rain.

Partly because of this accident and partly in order to relieve the fishing pressure on our small stretch of water at Sustut Lake, Craig, Sanderson, Fiorini and Davey Bob hiked down to the junction on Tuesday afternoon. There they stayed for the remaining four days of our trip. They found the water at the junction still very high and the fishing relatively poor.

Brian Magee and I, with Hunter Simpson and Dominic, stayed at Sustut Lake. Despite the continuing rains, we had excellent fishing, each taking one or more steelhead every day. When it rained too hard, we huddled in the remnants of our tent, and Brian gave me some fairly expensive lessons at gin rummy.

On Sunday at noon, the 15th day of our trip, the charter plane settled down on Sustut Lake right on schedule. Three hours later we were back in the town of Terrace and civilization. Soaking in a hot tub that evening for the first time in more than two weeks was a pleasure to remember.

Our total catch for the trip was about 100 steelhead, the smallest of which weighed 8 pounds, and largest 19 pounds. The aggregate weight of the catch was approximately 1,200 pounds. Except for the few we kept for eating all our fish were returned to the water. My score was 19 steelhead, the largest of which was 17 pounds. Of these fish I landed two on dry flies, twelve on regular wet flies, four on a small wet fly with a tiny golden spinner just above the hook, and one on spinning tackle.

My one steelhead taken on spinning tackle was the result of deliberate meat fishing. When the grizzly raided our camp for the second night in succession, he carried away our entire supply of meat—40 pounds of fresh goat and caribou meat. The next morning found us in real need of fish to eat. I borrowed Hunter Simpson's big spinning rod to be certain of taking at least one steelhead. On my second or third cast I had an 8 pounder which I horsed into the beach in not more than five minutes. Because it was no fun I switched back to my flyrod and took a second steelhead on a wet fly within the half hour.

Fishing on the Sustut revived my faith in the use of dry flies for steelhead. From my experiences on the Kispiox I had almost reached the conclusion that, during the fall runs, steelhead cannot be induced to rise to a dry fly. What I learned on the Sustut, however, was that the condition of the fish is the all-important factor rather than the actual date on the calendar. Unlike the Kispiox steelhead, the fish we caught on the Sustut and the Johanson were typical summer-run steelhead. They were sexually immature, bright in color, active in cruising around the pools and breaking water like ordinary rainbow trout.

Although I landed only two Sustut steelhead on dry flies, I had at least two dozen rises of fish that I failed to hook. Time and again, in the slow water just below Sustut Lake, I saw steelhead rise to my dry flies and then fail to seize the hook. At the time I was practically convinced that the frequent failure of these steelhead to strike was caused by fright at seeing the leader floating on the surface. Consequently, I tried using smaller leaders tapered down to a size of 2x. The result, however, was just the same. It was not until my visit to the Sustut in 1963 that I realized that this lazy rise and casual pass at a dry fly are generally characteristic of steelhead under such circumstances.

Gus Craig gave a beautiful demonstration one day of how to coerce a reluctant steelhead into rising to a dry fly. In a pool about half a mile below the junction he spotted a large steelhead lying in about four feet of water. He decided to fish for it with a dry fly, using the George Le Branche method of creating a hatch. For a solid half hour he cast over the fish with a Grizzly Wulff, attempting each time to put the fly in the same spot about 15 feet upstream from the steelhead and permitting it to drift freely right over the fish. After about the 30th successive cast he noticed his fish beginning to move its fins and to rise slightly in the water. Ten or fifteen casts later the big steelhead rose deliberately and took the fly. When Gus beached the fish, he found he had a 14 pounder.

For wet fly fishing I used only three kinds of flies. These were: the Skykomish, the Golden Girl, and Horner shrimp flies, all on hooks ranging from No. 4 to No. 8. When it seemed likely that the fish would take flies just under the surface I would use the unweighted Skykomish or Golden Girl. When it appears desirable to sink the fly deeply I would usually attach to my leader a weighted Horner Shrimp. Of the three, I had the most luck with the Skykomish, although I took steelhead on all three types.

From the luck enjoyed by Brian Magee and Ron Sanderson with a tiny spoon, it was apparent that the Sustut steelhead would come more readily to a flashing lure of this type than they would to any kind of fly. One morning I had an unusual visual demonstration of this fact. I was fishing alone in a large shallow pool about halfway between Sustut Lake and the lower bay. In the middle of the stream and lying in about four feet of water were 25 to 30 steelhead schooled up in a tight group. I waded into the stream as quietly as possible and took a position just below the school and about 25 feet away. In the gin clear water and the sun at the right angle I could see the fish almost as clearly as if they had been on the surface.

I started casting with a dry fly and for fifteen minutes drifted it over the school without any sign of reaction from the fish. I then shifted to a wet fly and made about a dozen casts with the same negative result. Just then Brian Magee appeared on the opposite bank and began casting with a small Gibb Stewart spoon.

When his first cast hit the water with a splash about 15 feet above the school, I could see every fish in the group become agitated. Their fins began to move and two steelhead darted out toward the lure for a few feet and then sank back. Exactly the same thing happened on the second cast. On the third cast one large steelhead streaked out and took the lure solidly. The ensuing battle, with several jumps and wild runs all over the pool, broke up the school and ended the fishing at this spot for the rest of the morning.

It certainly does not pay to be a purist in steelhead fishing. My usual practice on the Sustut was to take two rods out to the stream, one rigged with a floating line and a dry fly, and one with a sinking line and a wet fly. I would start fishing with the dry fly in the hope of inducing a rise before the pool had become disturbed. If the dry fly failed to produce, I would shift to the wet fly rod, and fish shallow at first and then deep. Finally, if I had no success, I would shift to my last resort, a small wet fly with a tiny spinner attached above the hook. This lure was much easier to cast with a fly rod than a small spoon, and almost equally effective.

The one real disappointment of our trip was our inability to fish the Sustut at its junction with the Bear River about 75 miles below Sustut

Lake. One reaches this spot by a 9 mile hike down the Bear River from Bear Lake. Gus Craig fished this water in 1958 and found there the best steelhead fishing in the whole area. He reported finding a succession of beautiful and easily wadeable pools, each of which was filled with steelhead. The high point of his experience was the taking of a 17 pound steelhead on a dry fly in a heavy snow storm. Our original itinerary in 1959 had included a trip to the Bear-Sustut Junction. We abandoned the plan, however, because of the continuous rains and high water. When the water became too high for satisfactory fishing on the upper Sustut we realized conditions would be even worse 75 miles further downstream.

The Sustut River gave me the finest steelhead fishing I had ever had in my life. It left me with an intense desire to return to Sustut Lake in order to fish the upper reaches of the river. The experience at Johanson Lake, however, was something different. The scenic beauty of Johanson is something I shall never forget, but the steelhead fishing was too poor to justify a second visit.

One final word of caution. This is no country for the individual who needs all the comforts of home on his fishing trips. This is a wild and rugged area and should be visited only in the company of thoroughly experienced guides. Living conditions are necessarily primitive, particularly if you happen to have a tent torn to shreds by a marauding grizzly. Waking up in an unheated tent at 20 degrees above zero and then washing in the icy water of the nearby stream is an experience that tends to separate the men from the boys.

———

I did return to Sustut Lake and the upper Sustut River in September 1963. The excursion turned out to be the most exciting and satisfactory fishing experience of my life.

My sole companion was Tom Cassady of Lake Forest, Illinois, who was one of the party that accompanied me to the Kispiox in 1959. Early in the morning of September 5th, Tom and I flew directly from Seattle with Buzz Fiorini in his Cessna 185 float plane, a distance of about 750 miles. Our only stop was at the town of Nanaimo, on Vancouver Island, where we cleared through the Canadian customs.

We put down on Sustut Lake early that same afternoon and were greeted there by our two white guides, Wally Love and Dallas Wookey. Wally, a brother-in-law of Jack Lee, had served as a guide for Cassady and me on the Kispiox in 1959, and again for me in 1961 when I made a trip to the Nass watershed. Tom and I had also become acquainted with Dallas on the Kispiox in 1959, where he was serving as a junior assistant at Jack Lee's camp. It was a joy to be with these two old friends, and I should like to add that I have never known two more competent, willing, and helpful guides. They both added greatly to the pleasure of our trip.

In contrast to the relatively primitive living conditions on the Sustut in 1959, we found on this latest visit that our guides, under the direction of Fiorini, had set up a very comfortable tent camp at a point where the lake flows into the river.

The reader will recall that the main body of Sustut Lake is separated from a wide shallow lower bay by a slowly meandering half-mile section of the river. This upper water contains several excellent holding pools for steelhead, all of which we had found packed with big fish in 1959. Our arrival in 1963, however, was ten days earlier in the month of September than that of our first visit. Consequently, we now found steelhead only in the lowest of these pools located at the entrance of the lower bay, and even here we found during the first few days of our trip a relatively small number of fish.

Again, as was the case in 1959, my first cast on the Sustut was with a large dry fly. The cast was a good one into the top of the bay pool and the Royal Wulff floated beautifully down through the riffle. In contrast to my experience in 1959, however, nothing happened to my first offering, and I was forced to make two more casts before I was rewarded by a slashing rise and strike. I had hooked a bright 10 pound steelhead which, after one big jump, dashed out into the bay, accompanied by all the other fish in the pool. I succeeded in beaching my fish after a battle of about 20 minutes, but almost two hours passed before the other steelhead, thoroughly spooked by the antics of my hooked fish, began to return timidly to the lower end of the pool.

Because the water was quite deep in this lower section, Cassady and I switched to the use of wet flies, which soon produced strikes for both of us. Tom succeeded in landing his fish, a bright 12 pounder, but I lost mine. My steelhead was a much larger fish, probably somewhere between 16 and 18 pounds, and made a run out into the bay which I was powerless to stop. When I saw the 200 yards of backing on my reel dwindle down to not more than 10 yards, I was forced to apply maximum pressure to the line. The result was a pull-out of the hook and a lost fish.

The following morning it was Cassady's turn to make the first cast into our one good pool. This cast produced a strike and another hooked steelhead, which Tom succeeded in landing. Again, all the other fish were spooked out of the pool and there were no more strikes for the balance of the morning.

Early that same afternoon I hooked and lost a steelhead on a pull-out of a dry fly, and left a wet fly on another fish's mouth when it broke my leader with a sudden unexpected jump. About an hour later Tom hooked a steelhead on a wet fly, and, during the ensuing battle, noticed my red streamer fly dangling from the jaw of his hooked fish. After landing and releasing this steelhead, Tom returned my fly to me. I promptly attached it to my leader and succeeded in landing another steelhead with it before the day ended.

Next morning, Saturday, it was again my turn to make the first cast with a dry fly. Less than a second after the fly hit the water it was greeted by a heavy splashing rise. Unfortunately, the steelhead missed the fly completely but the big splash was sufficient to spook all of the other fish in the pool. Almost immediately we saw the tell-tale wakes of a large number of big fish leaving the pool in a body.

The same annoying sequence of events recurred for Cassady on Sunday morning—a single cast, a rise, a missed fish, and the disappearance of all the steelhead. Since we had already started our trip down river to the camp at the junction of the Sustut and Johanson Creek we did not hang around to await the return of the fish to the pool.

At this point, after two and one-half days of fishing, Tom Cassady had landed seven steelhead, one on a dry fly and six on wet flies. My total was four, one on a dry fly and three on wet flies. To my chagrin I had also lost five good fish, four on pull-outs, one on a broken leader.

The six-mile trek down to the junction was accomplished by noon; the first three miles over the abominable muskeg, and the last three through a rain-drenched forest. Although I had travelled down and up this trail in 1959, to the surprise of everyone, including myself, I managed this time to get lost. About a mile short of the junction I was leading the procession and took a right fork in the trail, unseen by the others, and not realizing that it led up the bank of Johanson Creek and away from the junction.

Half an hour later I saw a stream ahead of me and hastened toward it in the confident expectation that I had reached the Sustut close to the junction. I then discovered that the stream I had reached was flowing not from the left to the right as anticipated but from the right to the left. I realized at once that I had stumbled onto Johanson Creek.

This discovery did not bother me in the slightest because I knew my destination was at the apex of the angle formed by the meeting of the two rivers, and that I could not possibly miss it if I followed the downstream course of either. Unfortunately, my peace of mind was not shared by our guides. When they reached the fallen log crossing on the Sustut and found no trace of me, Wally Love became almost frantic. Dropping his pack he dashed back up the trail, found my footprints at the fork, and caught up with me on Johanson Creek when I was still several hundred yards above the junction. It made me feel like a jackass to have caused him so much concern.

Incidentally, I saw the foot prints of more large wild animals on this section of the Johanson than I had ever seen before in any one area, and most of them were relatively fresh. I spotted the huge pad marks of several grizzlies, and the smaller marks of black bear; also the hoof prints of numerous caribou and moose. Finally, the surprisingly large pad marks of timber wolves were all over the place. I must add, however, that we failed to see any of these animals in the flesh during our six-day visit at the junction camp.

On our arrival we found the large pool at the junction teeming with at least 25 to 30 steelhead. After lunch Tom and I went into action. From this one pool during the afternoon I landed two good steelhead and lost two more on snags when following the fish downstream.

During the same period Cassady landed his daily limit of three steelhead. As a matter of fact, Tom bagged his limit of three fish on each of the six days we spent at the junction—a total of 18 fish—all taken on wet flies. In the same period, I landed only nine, also on wet flies, but lost at least an equal number, chiefly on snags and pull-outs. Tom's largest fish weighed 19 pounds while my largest reached 16 pounds.

Although an experienced woodsman and an accomplished fly fisherman, Tom had never previously caught a steelhead. As a result, we had a small joke at his expense on the afternoon of our arrival at Sustut Lake. When Tom appeared in his waders ready for fishing we noticed a tiny trout net dangling from his waist. After some persiflage we convinced him that such an implement would be worse than useless for landing huge steelhead. Buzz Fiorini then accompanied him to the river and quickly taught him the art of beaching these big fish. From this point on Cassady proved himself to be amazingly adept in hooking and landing steelhead. In addition, he was one of the most pleasant and considerate companions I have known on a stream.

The morning after our first exciting afternoon of fishing at the junction we moved downstream to the lower pools, extending for about a mile below the junction. In this stretch then were four good pools, all holding steelhead. The last and best of these was known to us as the Rock Pool which was just below a right angle turn in the river. Sheltered behind a huge boulder in the stream was a deep hole which in 1959 and again in 1963 we always found full of huge fish. Below this hole the pool sloped upward and widened to the tail more than 150 feet below the rock. Downstream from the pool the river extended for several hundred yards in a wide straight stretch which was a wonderful area for playing a hooked fish. On the near side of the stream was a wide gravel beach that made an ideal spot for casting. On the far side was a high bank from which our guides could spot for us all of the steelhead lying in the pool.

Despite the large aggregation of fish in the deep hole, most of the steelhead we caught at the Rock Pool were taken from the shallow water near the tail. I am sure that most of the latter were fresh arrivals at the pool that had not acquired the fortitude to join their larger fellows in the deep hole. I am also sure that most of the fish in the deep hole had been resting there for some time and had become relatively indifferent to the artificial lures that swept by them.

Moreover, it was exceedingly difficult to sink a wet fly deeply enough to reach the fish in the hole, because of the swiftness of the current beside the edge of the boulder. An upstream cast above the boulder would sweep down past the edge of the hole without entering it. A cast just below the boulder would be dragged downstream by the line before the fly had a chance to sink deeply. Despite those difficulties Tom succeeded in hooking and landing a 19 pound steelhead from this hole.

During the last two days of our stay at the junction, I managed to solve the problem of sinking a fly deeply into the hole. On the afternoon of Friday, the 13th, I crossed the river just below the tail of the pool. After working my way up along the high bank I entered the water several yards above the boulder. The current was very heavy and the water almost waist-deep, but I succeeded in reaching the security of the upstream side of the boulder. From this point of concealment I made a short cast with a Horner shrimp fly over the rock and quickly let out a lot of slack line.

The fly sank deeply into the hole and was promptly met by a solid strike. After two jumps my steelhead started a headlong dash downstream. Somehow I managed to get ashore and struggled down along the edge of the bank. After crossing the river below the pool, I succeeded in beaching a good 14 pound steelhead about three hundred yards downstream. Although I returned immediately to my position above the boulder, I had no more action the rest of the afternoon.

On Saturday morning I returned to the Rock Pool to try the same tactics. My second cast from behind the boulder was rewarded by an unusually heavy strike. Almost immediately an enormous dark steelhead came out of the water at a sharp angle right in my direction. It looked just like a huge torpedo broaching the surface of the ocean. The jump cleared the water by more than three feet and must have been at least ten feet in length. The resulting slack in my line enabled the fish to shake the fly loose as it hit the water. Although all such guesses are of doubtful validity, I am sure the steelhead was over 20 pounds. I shall never forget the ferocious appearance of this huge fish in its great leap for freedom. No more strikes occurred although I continued casting for another hour.

As the days succeeded one another at the lower camp, the productivity of the Junction Pool declined steadily. No more fish were to be found in the shallow water at the lower end; the few remaining steelhead were all packed in a tight group in the deep swift water at the head of the pool. Finally, on the morning of our departure we could not spot a single fish in the whole area. This showed us clearly that even in the case of migratory fish, no pool can stand a heavy beating for several days without being cleaned out. Although practically all of our fish were returned unharmed to the water, the steelhead must have realized that this was an unhealthy spot for them and proceeded to move on upstream.

We broke camp at noon on the 14th and hiked back to Sustut Lake. Buzz Fiorini had told us that the heavy run of steelhead always reached the upper pools just below the lake somewhere between the 12th and the 15th of September, and we were anxious to verify his prediction. When we arrived and found the pool at the entrance of the lower bay packed solidly with fresh steelhead, with countless more cruising around the bay, we were ready to agree that Sustut steelhead must have a calendar sense rivalling that of the swallows of Capistrano.

Then followed four days of the most amazing fishing of our lives. Saturday afternoon I fished alone at the bay pool and landed three bright steelhead on dry flies. To my surprise, the activity was almost continuous. No longer were the fish spooked out of the pool by the antics of a hooked fish. If some fish left the pool other fresh steelhead crowded in immediately. Almost every cast produced some kind of a rise. Most of these rises were of the lazy character described earlier in this chapter, the fish making casual swipes at the fly and frequently just bumping the fly with their noses. The only solution to this problem was to strike swiftly at the first sign of a rise, but even so I am sure that the ratio of rises to hooked fish during our last four days at Sustut Lake was at least five to one.

The evening Tom and I decided to take turns fishing alone at the bay pool, one taking it for the morning and the other for the afternoon.

Although there were now some fish in the upper pools, the fishing at the lower pool was so extraordinary that it seemed silly to waste much time on the others. On Sunday, Monday and Tuesday we each landed our daily quota of three steelhead, after not more than three hours of fishing apiece. All were taken on dry flies, and all but one, which Tom caught in the pool right at the camp, were hooked in the bay pool.

Since we were scheduled to fly back to civilization early Wednesday afternoon we were both anxious to make the most of our final morning of fishing. Tom had the first crack at the bay pool and landed his three steelhead on dry flies by 11:00 a.m. I then took over and beached two more good fish within an hour. For the next forty minutes, however, I had no more rises to my dry flies. About 12:40 p.m., I caught sight of our guide, Dallas, coming down the trail and I realized he had been asked to tell me that the time for our departure was at hand.

Since I was reluctant to end the trip without one more fish, I switched quickly to a wet fly. By the time Dallas reached my side I had already hooked a large dark steelhead. After about 20 minutes of short runs and jumps near the lower end of the pool, this big fish decided to take off across the bay. Realizing that I was operating on borrowed time, I maintained sufficient pressure on the line to prevent any long sustained runs. As a result, my steelhead pulled just like a bulldog, with an apparently endless series of hard, sharp tugs, each of which took out five to ten feet of my line. After about 30 minutes of this action, the fish was more than 200 yards out in the bay and I noticed that I had only a few more turns of backing on my reel. Fearing the loss of my fly line and leader, and feeling no diminution in the strength of the fish, I felt obliged to apply additional pressure. Almost immediately the line went slack. When I reeled in my 235 yards of line and backing, I discovered I had lost my last steelhead on a straight pull-out of the fly.

Our final score for the two weeks of fishing was a total of 64 steelhead landed, the smallest weighing 8 pounds and the largest 19 pounds. All of these fish were taken on flies, 28 with dry flies and 36 with wet flies. Cassady's total was 37 fish, 13 of which he took on dry flies. All of the fish landed conformed surprisingly to the pattern one would expect. Those taken on dry flies were relatively small, bright fish, running in weight from 8 to 12 pounds. All of the larger steelhead were hooked on wet flies and generally ran darker in color.

All but seven of these fish were returned unharmed to the stream. Of the seven retained, five were eaten and two carried back to Seattle as a gift to Mrs. Fiorini. We ate "Steelhead a la Sustut"—barbecued, broiled, and fried, prepared under the skillful direction of Buzz Fiorini. All of it provided magnificent eating.

The only dry flies we used were Royal Wulffs and Grizzly Wulffs, all on No. 6 hooks, and heavily dressed for use on Atlantic salmon. Our favorite wet fly was a small, scarlet deer hair streamer with silver foil around the shank. Also useful were the Skykomish Sunrise, and various types of Horner weighted shrimp flies.

During our stay on the Sustut the weather was good by usual northern British Columbia standards. Although we had some rain during practically every 24-hour period, most of it occurred at night and never once was sufficient to stop our fishing. Moreover, the precipitation did not cause any discoloration of the water or appreciable rise in the level of the stream. Until the last two days of our visit the temperature remained above freezing. During our last night at Sustut Lake, we had a fairly heavy snowfall and the next morning the water began to freeze in the guides of our rods. Perhaps we chose a good time to leave.

Although by now an old hand at steelhead fishing, I continued to be amazed by the power and vitality of these great fish. The explosive character of their jumps and the violence of their runs always startle me each time I experience them. It must be remembered that, by the time they reach Sustut Lake, these fish have journeyed some 400 miles upstream and have climbed over 4,000 feet above sea level. Yet their strength and endurance seems undiminished.

All in all, it was a most memorable trip. During the flight back to Seattle, Buzz told us that 64 big steelhead caught on flies in a two-week period was an unusual record, and that the taking of 28 of these fish on dry flies was something unheard of in the annals of steelhead fishing. He added that none of the veteran steelhead anglers of Seattle would believe the story unless confirmed by the sworn testimony of our guides.

VI *Other Streams in the Area*

THE BULKLEY RIVER is the largest tributary of the Skeena. After its junction with the Morice at Houston this big stream flows in a northwesterly direction for about 100 miles until it empties into the Skeena near Hazelton. In September of 1954 I spent three days fishing the Bulkley at several spots. The water was relatively low and crystal clear. Since I had found a fair number of steelhead in the lower Morice during the three preceding days of fishing there was good reason to hope that even more fish would be in the river 75 to 100 miles farther downstream.

Unfortunately this expectation failed to materialize. I hooked only one steelhead and saw no others. Oddly enough, the one steelhead I hooked rose to a dry fly. I was fishing one morning in a huge pool just below the falls at the Indian village of Old Moricetown. The whole pool was boiling with fish, mostly salmon, as they worked their way slowly up to the fish ladder at the side of the falls.

After trying various wet flies for more than two hours, I shifted to a large dry fly. This was a squirrel tail fly on a No. 6 hook, made by Pat Barnes of West Yellowstone and known as a "Sofa Pillow". It had proved effective for steelhead on the Upper Morice. Standing on a large boulder at the edge of the pool I started idly dapping the "Sofa Pillow" on the surface of the water about ten feet below me. Almost at once the fly was sucked quietly under the surface and I struck, thinking I had hooked a small fish.

Two seconds later, an enormous steelhead came straight out of the water just below me. He was so close I could see every mark on his glistening body. With dark green on his massive back and upper sides he was pure silver underneath, and with no sign of rainbow coloration anywhere. He was clearly a fresh run steelhead just in from the ocean. Even allowing for the fevered imagination of an excited fisherman, this fish must have weighed at least 20 pounds.

I scrambled quickly down from the boulder to the beach in order to have more space to maneuver. After two more tremendous leaps the big steelhead started on a run straight across the pool which was at least 200 yards wide at this point. I applied as much pressure as I dared and suddenly felt the line go slack. I reeled in, and the tell-tale curl at the end of the leader showed clearly the pull-out of the fly as a result of a faulty knot.

At Hunter Perry's suggestion, I was using for the first time an eight pound test leader made of German Platyl nylon. Hunter had warned me that this monofilament was so soft that it was necessary to tie an extra knot in the end of the leader before attaching the fly. This I had neglected to do, and the result was the loss of the most magnificent steelhead I have ever seen on the end of my line. I am sure the odds were heavily weighted against my landing this fish under any circumstances, because it would have been impossible to follow it downstream from the short stretch of beach where I was standing. Nevertheless, it was humiliating to realize I had lost this tremendous fish because of my own stupidity.

I know that the Bulkley has the reputation of being a great steelhead stream in the late fall and early winter. As previously mentioned, Buck Morris has written me of wonderful steelhead fishing in the Bulkley in mid-December. Unless it happened to be as low and clear, however, as I found it in 1954, I certainly could not recommend it for a fly fisherman. When I saw it in 1955 and again in 1959, the water in the Bulkley was high and dirty, and hopeless to fish with anything but a large flashing spoon.

The big Skeena itself, of course, carries vast quantities of steelhead during the fall and winter but is no stream for fly fishing. I have never seen this big body of water when it was not either slate gray with glacial silt or brown with mud. I have tried fishing the Skeena at various spots all the way from the mouth of the Babine to a point several miles below the town of Terrace. The net result of these attempts was one Dolly Varden trout and two male humpback salmon. I am sure that one would have better luck finding a needle in a haystack than to hope that a steelhead would make contact with a small fly in this water. Of course, it could happen but it would be luck if it did.

There are many other small tributaries of the Skeena which I have never fished. Amongst those reported to have good fall runs of steelhead are: the Telkwa River, the Copper River, and the Lakelse River. All three are relatively short streams and are located close to towns. The Telkwa enters the Skeena a short distance upstream from Smithers, the Copper just above Terrace, and the Lakelse flows out of a lake by the same name and joins the Skeena a short distance below Terrace. I suspect that all three of these streams are well crowded with fishermen from the nearby towns when the runs are on.

Buzz Fiorini tells me that, from the air, he has seen large numbers of steelhead in several of the small tributaries of the Skeena in the area north of the Sustut. The difficulty is that, in the absence of any nearby lakes large enough for a float plane to land and take off, these streams are relatively inaccessible. It would be great fun to spend a couple of weeks exploring them in a large helicopter, and perhaps some day I shall do it.

THE NASS

The Nass River is not part of the Skeena watershed, since it flows directly into the Pacific about 50 miles north of the mouth of the Skeena. The two watersheds run closely parallel all the way up to their respective sources in the rugged mountains some 200 miles to the north. In many places the tributaries of these two streams are within a few miles of each other.

Knowing that the Nass has the reputation of being a fine steelhead river I became interested some years ago in exploring its possibilities. Since I was advised that this stream, in its lower reaches, is even dirtier than the Skeena, it was obvious that the only hope of finding good water for fly fishing must be in the headwaters of the tributaries.

The Nass valley is even more remote than the Skeena, and, to the best of my knowledge, there are no permanent human habitations any-where in the entire watershed.

Finally in 1961 I persuaded my three Canadian friends, Craig, Magee, and Sanderson to join me in a trip to the upper Nass. We established our base camp on Domdochax Lake about 50 miles west of the junction of the Sustut and Skeena rivers. Damdochax Creek flows out of the little lake and joins the Nass about 12 miles farther west. We flew in on September 12, and spent the next two weeks in the area.

Damdochax Creek is a narrow, swift stream with a heavy growth of overhanging trees and bushes on both banks. For the first half mile below the lake, we found good dry fly fishing for small rainbow trout. Farther downstream, however, we found no fish of any kind.

Until the last two days of our visit we saw no steelhead. Then, without warning, steelhead began to appear in Damdochax Creek. Dur-ing these last 48 hours our party landed five fair-sized steelhead. It was clear that the run was just beginning. If we had been able to stay on for another week I am sure we would have hooked many more of these big fish. Because of the confines of the stream, however, Damdochax Creek is not satisfactory water for steelhead fishing.

During our stay, Buzz Fiorini and I made several exploratory trips in his plane to other parts of the upper Nass watershed. We followed the Nass proper right to its source in a small mountain lake. We found it heavily silted and dirty throughout its entire course. We then followed the Bell-Irving River, the largest tributary of the Nass, all the way down from its source. We found it even dirtier than the Nass. Except for Damdochax Creek, the only clear stream we discovered was the Kwinageese River which flows into the Nass about 60 miles southwest of Damdochax Lake. From the air this stream looked so difficult to get into that we never explored its fishing potential. As far as I am concerned, anyone else who wants it can have the entire Nass watershed.

ARCTIC GRAYLING

On one of our exploratory trips Buzz and I flew all the way north to the Dease River just short of the Yukon boundary. The Dease

River, which has its source in Dease Lake, is part of the Mackenzie watershed that flows into the Arctic Ocean. Here I had my first taste of fishing for arctic greyling. In two hours we landed about a dozen of these small fish on dry flies. They ran in size from about twelve to sixteen inches. Fishing for greyling proved to be fairly good sport, chiefly because the strike is so light and quick that one's reactions have to be very fast to hook them.

When we finished fishing, we realized it was too late of a murky afternoon to get back to our base camp before dark. In addition to our fishing tackle and waders, we had on board the plane only our sleeping bags and a bottle of Scotch whiskey. We decided to try to find bed and board at a small settlement of houses at the southern end of Dease Lake, planning to employ the Scotch whiskey as an instrument of barter.

When we landed at the settlement, we found it completely deserted except for one lone man, and a small dog of uncertain parentage. The man, a Scots Canadian, was a mechanic for a helicopter that was based at this point. We knew him only as Scotty, and we learned that after a long summer at this God forsaken spot he was about to return to Vancouver for the winter. He seemed delighted with our company and readily agreed to provide us with supper, bed and break-fast. We in turn agreed to share our Scotch.

Just as we were getting settled in Scotty's tiny cabin on the side of a steep hill, several other individuals began to drift in. First came the helicopter pilot, a fine looking negro from Los Angeles. Then arrived a stout and elderly Belgian prospector. Finally, we were startled by the arrival of a handsome, young Scotsman of the British Columbia Forestry Service, who bore the distinguished name of Douglas Hamilton. A more mixed bag I have never seen.

Aided by the Scotch and a bottle of cognac produced by the helicopter pilot, we had one of the most hilarious evenings I can remember. After dinner, Scotty perched himself on a high window sill, with a plaid cap on one side of his head, and led us all in singing Scottish ballads. This continued until the small hours of the morning before we finally turned in. The next day we flew back soberly to our camp on Damdochax Lake.

VII   *Fishing Methods for Steelhead*

THE FEEDING HABITS of steelhead after their return to fresh water present a baffling problem, for which no one seems to have any complete answer. Sufficient evidence is available, however, to enable one to arrive at some limited conclusions. That summer steelhead do some feeding in fresh water there can be no doubt, but it appears quite unlikely that such feeding occurs with any regularity or is sufficient in amount to provide any real nourishment for fish the size of steelhead.

I have examined the stomachs of a considerable number of steelhead taken in various parts of the Skeena Valley. Only in a few of those caught on the Upper Morice, where the insect life is unusually abundant, have I found any appreciable amount of food. In those taken on the Sustut there was no evidence of food whatsoever. The stomachs of two of these latter fish, however, did contain a single aspen leaf which must have been gulped down by mistake and then remained undigested.

In response to my inquiries, I have received some very interesting observations from three students of this subject. From Les Cox, game warden at Smithers, came the following comments:

"In connection with the feeding habits of these fish, I too have noticed that some have food in their stomachs while others do not. Do you think the answer may lie with the determination of these creatures to get to the spawning area without undue delay and then take some nourishment if such is available? An example of that would be the Morice River run. The Bulkley River is usually choked with ice jams in the early winter, sometimes as early as November. Yet the Morice River is often open all winter. I do believe that the steelhead with the greatest distance to travel are the first to start up the river."

Vic Giraud, Fishery Officer at Prince Rupert, wrote me as follows: "I have little to add to your remarks on feeding habits. I have examined a number of steelhead in the system and have found that very few stomachs contained food. A few that I examined on the lower Skeena contained a little food, only a trace, and not enough to identify. Mr. A. J. Hipp, a friend of mine at Lakelse Lake, reported steelhead with stomachs full of salmon eggs in late October and early November from Lakelse River. A good run of spawning cohoe were on the grounds at the time, and no doubt the steelhead picked up the loose eggs. This is the only instance of definite steelhead feeding in fresh water that I have proof of."

The clearest and most comprehensive statement of the problem came to me recently in a letter from Roderick Haig-Brown, from which I quote the following:

"I was much interested in your letter of November 17. I have certainly found food in steelhead stomachs, though rarely in great quantity. The summer before last I caught a small summer fish (about 2½ pounds) on the Gold River with five full-grown dragonflies in its stomach (they were large, *Aeschna* or that general type). Other small fish of up to about this size (but not, I think much larger) often have fair quantities of caddis or snails evidently scraped off the rocks, which indicate very positive feeding."

"I described some 'feeding' of winter fish in *The Western Angler*. I particularly remember one good-sized fish, caught on falling water after a high freshet, which had a stomach full of salmon roe.

"Apart from instances of very small fish (2½ pounds and less) I do not think any of this really constitutes feeding. It is rather a matter of opportunity tripping the latent feeding reaction in the fish, and this can be done by natural or artificial offerings. Another complication that probably has bearing is the return of river surroundings which may well reawaken freshwater habits acquired in the first two years; this would account for the surprising response to dry flies. I feel sure that the winter fish with the belly full of salmon roe was responding merely to opportunity, because I have caught several that had taken large numbers of preened out merganser or goldeneye feathers—these presumably would have been rolling down close to bottom as were the salmon eggs after the freshet."

"There are several reasons why I can't believe in any serious, necessary feeding by steelheads and these are some of them: (1) The inconsistency. So many fish have nothing at all in them or merely one or two bugs when a lot more feed than that is available if they went after it. (2) Many, if not most, summer steelhead streams, do not begin to produce feed in quantities that would make any real difference to such large fish. (3) The general proposition that migratory salmonoid runs are established by evolutionary selection and the members of those runs have enough stored body fats to take care of freshwater migration, waiting period and spawning activities without serious feeding. Obviously none of these arguments is conclusive; but to me, taken with the observed habits of the fish, they are convincing. Why small maturing fish should feed actively while the larger ones do not, I am not sure. But I think it may well be because they are less removed from their freshwater life and so resume it more readily."

Certain it is that the instinct to feed remains alive in steelhead after they enter fresh water. However dormant this instinct may be, it is still sufficiently strong to cause steelhead to react under the right circumstances to both wet and dry flies. The fish most likely to react positively to artificial lures are the summer-run, or sexually immature steelhead. When the spawning period is close at hand, and the milt sac of the male and the egg sac of the female have become too swollen to permit the digestion of food, steelhead are much less likely to be interested in simulations of insect life. If they strike at a deeply sunken wet fly, or a flashing spoon, I suspect it is because of irritation or anger rather than because of any desire to feed. Under such circumstances, the reaction of steelhead would appear to be similar to that of Pacific salmon at or near their spawning grounds.

The ideal situation for the use of dry flies on steelhead is when they are cruising around a pool close to the surface, and breaking water just like any other rainbow trout. They can also be induced to rise to dry flies when you find them lying in water not more than four to five feet beneath the surface. As mentioned previously, Gus Craig gave a beautiful demonstration of coercing a steelhead to rise to a dry fly under such circumstances by "creating a hatch". If you find steelhead lying at the bottom of a deep pool, you will certainly waste your time casting to them with a dry fly.

When I fish for steelhead with a dry fly, I use exactly the same technique that I would in casting for any other type of trout. I try to get into a position about twenty feet below the fish and well off to one side. I then use a "slack line" or "curve" cast so as to permit as long a free drift of the fly as possible. I try to make the fly light on the water about ten to fifteen feet above the fish and then drift right over their noses. Although a long free drift is usually desirable, I have taken a number of steelhead that struck the dry fly after it started to drag across the current at the end of the drift.

Because steelhead in slow, clear water are the spookiest fish I have ever known, every precaution should be taken to avoid disturbing them. You should work your way to your casting position as slowly and quietly as possible, and then make each cast as deliberately and carefully as you can. You should use a long, light leader, not less than 9 to 10 feet in length, and tapered down to not more than 0x. Although I have landed some steelhead on dry flies with leaders tapered down as small as 2x, I have lost a considerable number on such light leaders. Experience has finally taught me that, if properly presented, an 0x tippet attached to a dry fly is not likely to frighten rising steelhead.

I had one vivid illustration of just how spooky steelhead can be in slow, clear water. I was fishing one morning with Brian Magee in the pool just above the outlet to the lower bay of Sustut Lake. We both started casting from the right bank to about a dozen steelhead that we could see lying in the center of the fairly shallow pool. I suddenly decided to cross the stream and try fishing from the other bank. In order not to disturb the fish I stepped back quietly into the woods and worked my way upstream to a point at least 50 yards above the head of the pool. Immediately after I had entered the water to wade across, Brian shouted to me that every fish in the pool had darted into the bay. That ended our fishing for the morning in that particular pool.

My experiences on the Sustut in September, 1963, gave me fresh insight into the limitations as well as the possibilities in the use of dry flies for steelhead. There can be no doubt that, in landing 28 of these fish on surface lures. Tom Cassady and I were blessed by an unusually favorable set of circumstances. A great mass of fresh steelhead, crowd-ing into a shallow pool with a slow moving current, provided con-ditions that would be difficult to duplicate. The constant succession of rises, most of which were lazy and accompanied by casual swipes at the fly, convinced me that these fish were responding to a dormant instinct and were not particularly interested in active feeding.

On a great many occasions, however, in a wide variety of un-disturbed pools, my first or second cast with a dry fly has resulted in a solid strike. Then followed either no more rises or a series of the lazy rises described above. This fact makes me believe that these half-hearted strikes were due at least in part to uneasiness of the fish after the pool had been disturbed.

That the use of surface lures for steelhead is a highly effective method under proper conditions is shown by the fact that at least half of some 80 of these fish I have landed in the Skeena Valley rose to dry flies. For a while this accomplishment gave me the false illusion that I was practically the discoverer of this method of steelhead fishing. I now realize, of course, that such is not the case. Nevertheless, I am sure that less than one percent of the thousands of fishermen who pursue steelhead every fall have ever hooked one with a dry fly.

Surprising as it may seem, the extensive literature on steelhead fishing contains only the barest mention of the use of dry flies. Clark Van Fleet, in his substantial book, "Steelhead to a Fly"*, devotes one brief paragraph to the subject. John Atherton, in his charming little book, "The Fly and the Fish"†, never ever mentions it. Roderick Haig-Brown‡ is probably the greatest living expert on steelhead. Yet even he admits it is only within the past few years that he has discovered that summer steelhead will rise more readily to dry flies than they will to wet.

---

* Clark C. Van Fleet: *Steelhead to a Fly*, Little Brown & Company, 1951.
† John Atherton: *The Fly and the Fish*, The MacMillan Co., 1951.
‡ Roderick Haig-Brown: *Fisherman's Summer*, William Morrow & Co., 1959.

The only writer I have come across to whom dry fly fishing for steelhead seems to be "old hat" is Frank R. Steel. In his excellent little book, "Fly Fishing"§ he writes:

"I fished almost entirely in this standard way (a wet fly cast down-stream and across, fished by the action method) the first season I was fishing for steelhead. As I lived on the Umpqua and Rogue Rivers for a number of years, I gradually tried modifications of all the trout fishing methods on steelhead. In the right conditions, they all work. I have taken a lot of steelhead on a dry fly—some up to 22 pounds. I have taken them with a wet fly fished upstream by the natural drift method. That is very effective."

The net of this is that the use of dry flies for steelhead is still in its infancy. I am confident that this technique will become increasingly popular as its possibilities are recognized by fly fishermen who angle primarily for pleasure rather than for meat. It should be clear from our earlier discussions that successful dry fly fishing can be expected only in the case of summer-run steelhead. Such fish have behavior characteristics very similar to those of resident rainbow trout. I have never heard of winter-run steelhead rising to dry flies, and it seems most unlikely that it should occur.*

In using wet flies for steelhead the traditional method is to cast across the current at a downstream angle, and then give action to the fly either by raising and lowering the tip of the rod, or by the use of a slow hand-twist retrieve. For myself, I greatly prefer the technique of casting a wet fly at an upstream angle and then mending the line as soon as the fly hits the water. In this manner you permit the fly to sink deeply during the relatively long free drift. I have found that a wet fly rising toward the surface when the drag commences is particularly deadly for steelhead, as well as for all other types of trout.

The upstream cast seems to be equally effective whether you are fishing for steelhead lying fairly close to the surface or whether you are trying to reach fish at the bottom of a deep pool. In the latter

§ Frank R. Steel: *Fly Fishing*, Paul, Richmond & Company, 1946, p. 115.
*Any sweeping generalization about fish or fishing is always dangerous. Thus, it is highly probable that I shall hear from some fisherman before long who has taken a winter steelhead on a dry fly.

case, however, you would be well advised to use a weighted fly in order to be certain that your lure sinks deeply enough. It would appear essential to employ the upstream cast when angling for winter-run fish. If you are to have any chance at all of attracting a winter steelhead to a fly, it is necessary for the lure almost to drag along the bottom of the stream.

It seems clear to me that steelhead go through successive periods of activity and inactivity. When active the fish move upstream and are likely to cruise around and break water like resident rainbows. When such fish first enter a holding pool, they can usually be found in the shallow water near the tail. Under these conditions, they will be responsive either to wet or dry flies.

When steelhead settle down into a deep hole, however, they are undoubtedly resting and tend to become lethargic. These periods of inactivity may last for days and usually cause great frustration to the fly fisherman. A first or second cast with a deeply sunken wet fly may produce a strike but you can be certain no more strikes will follow unless the pool is rested for several hours. Instead of scattering, the steelhead merely settle more deeply into the hole and ignore all subsequent offerings. It is possible, of course, to dredge a steelhead out of a deep hole after it has been disturbed by constant casts with a flashing piece of hardware, but I suspect that the fish strike at such lures merely as a result of prolonged irritation. One final and obvious comment is that one is more likely to find the darker and sexually mature steelhead at the bottom of deep holes, and the brighter (and usually smaller) fish in shallower water.

In striking steelhead I do so exactly as I would any other trout. Although I have read in several places of the desirability of a delayed strike with steelhead, I have never found this to be the case either with wet or with dry flies. I have had plenty of trouble conditioning myself to a delayed strike in wet fly fishing for Atlantic salmon, but never in the case of steelhead. Only once have I been definitely aware of making a premature strike for a steelhead. This was the instance reported in the chapter on the Morice River when I was fishing with a dry fly from an anchored boat. I struck and completely missed a rising steelhead. The big fish then charged in and took the fly on the surface within five feet of the boat. It is possible also that at times I have hooked steelhead insecurely by too swift a strike with a wet fly. I have lost a few steelhead as a result of a pull-out of the fly but the number has been small, and I have no idea if a slower strike would have prevented these losses.

One elementary principle in handling steelhead or Atlantic salmon is always to play the fish directly on the reel. If you attempt to strip in line with your free hand, you are almost certain to suffer a break in your tackle, and you may also run the risk of losing a finger. The moment a steelhead strikes, reel in your slack line as quickly as possible and then never touch the line with your free hand. Once I placed the forefinger of my free hand on the line in an effort to slow down the run of the steelhead and received a burn at the first joint almost down to the bone. Of course, you may tighten or loosen the drag on the reel as your judgment dictates, but *keep your hand off the line*.

In playing steelhead I always hold my rod as high as my reach will permit and only lower the tip when the fish jumps. As I feel the fish beginning to tire, I gradually tighten the drag. This latter should be done with caution, however, because even a tired steel-head can react with sufficient violence to break the leader if the drag is too tight.

After my first few experiences with steelhead I abandoned permanently the use of a landing net. I reached this conclusion after the ludicrous experience of attempting to force a 13 pound steelhead into a small trout net. Three times I managed to get half the body of the big fish into the net and three times it flopped out when I started to lift the net from the water. I finally succeeded in beaching the fish by kicking it up on the gravel bank.

If you have an open beach, it is a relatively simple matter to land a steelhead without the use of a net or any other aid. The thing to do, once you see your fish is exhausted, is to back slowly up the beach with your rod held high. As the steelhead comes into the shallow water it will start flopping, and, under the steady pressure of the line, will usually flop itself right up on the shore. If no open beach is available the best way to land a steelhead is simply to reach down with your free hand, get a firm grip around the gill plates and lift the fish out of the water.

If you happen to have a guide at hand with an oversize net there is, of course, no harm in having him use it. Better still, if you feel the need of some aid in landing steelhead, I would recommend the use of a Lee Wulff Tailer. This is a spring wire loop at the end of a short pole. The expanded loop is slipped over the tail of the fish and then sprung shut. With a tight noose around the body above the tail, it is a simple matter to pull the fish ashore. This method is very effective in landing Atlantic salmon, and I see no reason why it should not work equally as well with steelhead.

TACKLE

For a number of years I suffered from the delusion that the most expert fly fishermen always used the lightest and smallest rods. Doubtless this notion came from watching movies of Lee Wulff taking huge Atlantic salmon on a 1¾-ounce, 6 foot rod. As a result, when I first visited the Skeena Valley, I fished entirely with a 3½-ounce, 7-foot rod.

The big, turbulent streams of the Northwest soon taught me some wisdom and humility. I learned to agree with Edward Hewitt's conclusion that the use of extremely light tackle for big fish in large streams is nothing other than a *tour de force*. Tiny rods are for little fish and small streams. Moreover, a large reel, which is a necessity for steelhead or salmon, attached to a small light rod, gives you a combination that is entirely out of balance.

At the other extreme, I have a strong prejudice against the huge, two handed rods still widely used by British fishermen. I have found them very clumsy to handle, and not necessary on any streams I have ever fished either for steelhead or Atlantic salmon. I am sure there are streams where such equipment is necessary. My friend, Al Swinnerton of San Francisco, advised me that the Alta in Norway is just such a river. The swiftness of the current, the huge wet flies used, and the large size of the salmon all combine to dictate the use of unusually large and powerful tackle. It is only under such a set of circumstances, however, that I would concede the desirability of employing these old-fashioned "telegraph poles".

From my own experience, what I want in a steelhead or salmon rod is a single-handed weapon that is long enough, and has enough backbone to cast a long fly, and also to exert some control over a hooked fish. On the other hand, it must not be so heavy as to leave me exhausted after a day of fishing. These characteristics I have found best exemplified in the bamboo rods manufactured by E. C. Powell of Marysville, California. I realize, of course, that every fly fisherman has his own pet rod maker, and I have no desire to start an argument with the champions of the many other fine rods now available. It just happens that, for power and action at a given weight, I would choose Powell rods over any I have ever tried.

I own several of these rods, but my favorites for steelhead and Atlantic salmon are two that weigh 5¼-ounces each, and are 9½ feet in length. One is a two-piece rod with fairly stiff action and unusual power for its weight. The other is a three-piece rod with a somewhat softer action. For my particular strength and fishing abilities these rods are ideal for both steelhead and Atlantic salmon. I can fish with them throughout a long day without undue fatigue. With either rod one can easily cast a fly 80 to 90 feet, and I find that I can control the line and a hooked fish much more efficiently than I can with a shorter and lighter rod.

In addition to steelhead, I have used these rods successfully on bonefish, small tarpon, and Atlantic salmon. In fact, my wife killed a 34 pound salmon on the Restigouche River with one of these rods.

In place of a detachable butt piece, I use an ordinary rubber bicycle grip. I jam it tightly over the butt-end of the rod and rest it against my chest when fighting a heavy fish. The three inches of additional length given to the butt by the bicycle grip are sufficient to permit free action of the reel.

My knowledge of steelhead flies is limited, and my tastes in this connection are quite simple. Fly fishing in the swift water of the big rivers of the Northwest does not require the delicacy of judgment in the choice of flies that may be called for elsewhere. Thus, I am sure that an exact "matching of the hatch" is desirable on the slow-moving, chalk streams of England, but it would certainly be a waste of time in the Skeena Valley. Instead, the size and buoyancy of dry flies seems much more important than their shape and color. In the case of wet flies, a wide variety can be used successfully as long as they are bright and flashing in appearance.

What you need primarily in a surface lure is a fairly large fly that floats high in the water and will also take a lot of beating. I have found the Wulff deer-hair flies so satisfactory in these respects that I use practically nothing else for steelhead. These flies have great buoyancy, and, with a moderate amount of fly dressing, will stand up under a lot of punishment. I usually obtain the best results with these flies on No. 6 and No. 8 hooks, although I have taken some steelhead on hooks as small as No. 12. I have never found, however, that it made the slightest difference to steelhead what color pattern was used in these deer-hair dry flies. I have also had some success in the past with large, squirrel-tail dry flies, but have practically given up using them because of their tendency to become soggy after a short period of fishing.

In the case of wet flies for steelhead fishing, the most important distinction is between the weighted and unweighted types. In the unweighted category there are many different varieties that can be used successfully. Most of these are brightly colored streamers or bucktails on hooks ranging from No. 4 to No. 8. I happen to have had the most luck with the Skykomish Sunrise, the Golden Girl, and Polar Shrimp flies. Since all three of these are standard steelhead patterns, it seems unnecessary to present a detailed description of them in these pages.

In the category of weighted flies, I have used only the lightly weighted Optic flies, and the more heavily weighted Horner Shrimp flies. Both of these types are large deer-hair streamers, the hair being dyed bright orange or bright red. The Horner Shrimp has silver colored wire wrapped around the shank of the hook, while the lighter Optic has merely a hook, with a heavy silvered shank.

Weighted flies, of course, are clumsy to cast and put a certain amount of strain on a rod. I also discovered last season another hazard in the use of weighted flies. While fishing the Upper Sustut, I was attempting a long cast with a Horner Shrimp. On its forward flight, the heavy fly struck the tip of my rod and broke it off about six inches from the end. For these reasons I prefer to use unweighted flies except where it is necessary to sink the lure very deeply.

Just as is the case with fly rods, there are many excellent makes of reels available for fly fishermen. My own preference, however, in steelhead or salmon fishing is for the Hardy "St. John". I like a single-action reel, and I have found those produced by Hardy to be unusually rugged and dependable. The "St. John" has a 3⅞-inch barrel, which is large enough to hold 200 yards of backing in addition to the fly line. I use a 12 pound test nylon backing known as a "squidding line". The small diameter of this line makes it easy to accommodate 200 yards of backing on the reel and still leave room for a large sized fly line.

I still have in my possession a good supply of gut leaders, but I have not used any of them for several years. Platyl nylon is so much stronger for a given diameter, and has become so uniform in quality that I can see no reason for using anything else. I prefer to make my own leaders and always carry with me coils of Platyl monofilament in a wide range of sizes. I start at the top with a length of 20 pound test material, which is spliced permanently to the end of the fly line. This splice assures a smooth passage of the joint through the guides of the rod. Then, by the use of a series of barrel knots, it is easy to taper the leader down to any degree of fineness and to any length that may be desired.

For the use of dry flies and nymphs on ordinary rainbow trout, I have found that a Platyl tippet as small as 5x or 6x can be handled satisfactorily. For steelhead and Atlantic salmon with wet flies, I ordinarily use a tippet which has a test strength of 12 pounds. In the case of dry fly fishing, my tippets are tapered down to 0x, or 8.5 pounds test for angling in slow water and to 10 pounds test for use in swift water. Under no circumstances do I ever use a leader of greater test strength than 12 pounds, because, if a break occurs, I wish to be certain that it takes place in the leader rather than in my backing which has only a 15 pound test.

Now, to conclude this chapter, I have a few words to say about wading equipment. Stocking foot, chest waders with separate wading shoes have always seemed the most satisfactory to me. On the other hand, I have never liked the waders made of rubberized cloth, even the so-called lightweight product of British design. They always bind me in the legs and are clumsy and tiresome to walk in for any distance.

The result is that I have experimented with practically every type of light plastic wader that has come to market during the past 15 years. Unfortunately, all of the earlier models would snag, puncture or tear on the drop of a hat. I found myself spending almost as much time with a patch kit as I did on a stream. Recently, however, considerable improvement has been made in this type of wader. The Hodgman waders, especially, are much more durable than the earlier models, although I have had trouble even with these from splitting at the seams. I have just purchased a new pair of Hodgman nylon waders which are very light in weight and are reported to be unusually durable.

Another type of wader I have found quite satisfactory is a light rubber product known as "Totes". The rubber stretches easily and, as a result, the waders fit snugly around the feet and have no binding effect on the legs. Until I visited the Sustut River I was convinced they were very difficult to snag or tear. In the rough undergrowth of this area, however, I soon produced a tear in each leg. After a quick and fairly easy repair job I tried the experiment of wearing a pair of blue jeans over the waders. With this protection I had no more trouble with snags. Except in very rough country I still consider "Totes" the most satisfactory lightweight waders I have ever used.

In wading shoes my preference is for the felt-soled basketball type of shoe made by United States Rubber Co. They are light in weight, last well, and are easy to resole with extra felts. This factor of lightness of weight of all wading equipment is important to my mind when wading in streams with heavy currents. If you slip in over your depth, as I have on a couple of occasions, your chances of getting ashore are considerably improved if you are wearing light, non-binding waders and lightweight shoes.

Many fishermen profess to dislike plastic and rubber waders because of their tendency to produce excessive perspiration. For myself, this factor is an asset rather than a liability. I always start a fishing trip with some excess weight around the midriff and am delighted to watch it melt away under the pressure of strenuous exercise, aided by perspiration under my waders.

*Bobby Fennelly and guide Jimmie with 32-pound salmon
which she killed on the Restigouche River*

Author with hide of goat shot on range above Morice Lake

VIII *Steelhead and Atlantic Salmon*

STEELHEAD HAVE BEEN called "The Atlantic Salmon of the North-west" and many writers have commented on the similarity in characteristics and habits of these two great game fish. For many years this subject has fascinated me, and on all my trips after one or the other of these fish, I have attempted to observe and note the minor differences between the two as well as the broad similarities. I certainly cannot qualify as an expert on Atlantic salmon but I have fished for them with considerable success in New Brunswick, Nova Scotia, Newfoundland, and Iceland.

Steelhead and Atlantic salmon are both anadromous fish. The eggs of each species are deposited and fertilized by the parents in the rivers of their birth. When the offspring emerge from the eggs they remain in fresh water from one to three years before migrating to the ocean. After from one to four years of the rich feeding available in salt water, steelhead and Atlantic salmon return to fresh water to spawn. At this stage both types are many times larger than when they first entered the ocean. Almost invariably each steelhead and each salmon returns not only to the river of its birth but to the particular tributary of that river where it first saw the light of day. No one has solved the mystery of this homing instinct, but that it does exist has been proven by countless tests.

As previously noted, all Pacific salmon die immediately after spawning. Both steelhead and Atlantic salmon, on the other hand, do not die automatically after spawning. A considerable but unknown percentage of each species continues to live and returns to the ocean. A fairly small percentage of each comes back later to fresh water for a second spawning.

Atlantic salmon usually spawn in the late fall, while steelhead usually spawn in the late winter and early spring. The resulting difference in the sexual maturity of the two species at any given time of the year may account for some minor variations in their respective habits.

We have already discussed in some detail the feeding habits of steel-head in fresh water. In substance there is clear evidence of some feeding by steelhead after their return to the river, but such feeding is certainly sporadic and small in amount.

In the case of Atlantic salmon, it has long been the cherished belief of most of the experts that these fish cease feeding entirely soon after reaching fresh water. For myself I am no longer willing to accept this dictum as gospel. Mounting evidence seems to indicate that Atlantic salmon continue to feed sporadically in a manner practically identical with that of steelhead.

An excellent article on this subject by Dana S. Lamb has appeared recently.* Mr. Lamb presents many convincing instances of actual feeding by salmon after their return to the river. His attitude is well summed up by an excerpt which he cites from a British writer: ". . . if anglers were not so slavish in believing everything that was written in the past and since constantly rehashed—such as salmon not taking *any* food in fresh water because their stomachs are out of action (incorrect)—they would not be so conservative and unwilling to vary technique".†

My own observations lead me to support the same conclusion. While fishing for salmon in Iceland I had a vivid illustration of how eagerly these fish will take worms while refusing to look at any kind of fly. After this experience, no one could convince me that salmon lose all interest in feeding in fresh water. Moreover, I learned on the same trip that Atlantic salmon, like steelhead, will come more readily to a brightly flashing spoon than they will to an ordinary fly. The prohibition of the

* Dana S. Lamb, *On Salmon Feeding in Fresh Water* — Bulletin of The Anglers Club of New York, June 1960.
† L. N. R. Gray, *The Field*, June 22, 1959.

use of live bait and all artificial lures, except wet and dry flies, on most North American salmon streams has undoubtedly been a factor in keeping alive for so long in the United States the traditional belief that these fish do not feed.

Fortunately, however, Atlantic salmon, as well as steelhead, will usually come to wet and dry flies with sufficient enthusiasm to make the sport attractive to fly fishermen. In each case the dry fly is likely to be more effective when the water is low and clear, and the wet fly more effective when the water is high.

Being notorious traditionalists, most fly fishermen dislike experiment' ing with untested lures when they can use flies of proven effectiveness. For example, shortly before World War I, a group of pioneers, including such men as Hewitt, La Branche, and Monell, made the exciting discovery that dry fly fishing for Atlantic salmon was more effective in low, clear water than the use of wet flies. Nevertheless, many years had to elapse before the dry fly technique became generally popular with salmon fishermen.

A similar situation now exists in the case of steelhead. It is only within the past few years that any but a rare few steelhead fishermen have appreciated the possibilities of taking summer steelhead on dry flies. Even now this knowledge is limited to a very small fraction of the large numbers who fish for steelhead every year. I venture to predict that many more years will pass before the use of dry flies becomes widespread amongst steelhead fishermen.

Also, I am sure that there is nothing magic about the beautiful, and expensive wet flies for salmon usually produced in Great Britain. Lee Wulff has told me he has found many ordinary trout flies at least equally as effective. Already the dry flies used for both steelhead and salmon are completely interchangeable. Some day I intend to try some of the brighter varieties of salmon wet flies on steelhead. I can see no reason why they should not take these fish.

Reference has been made above to my salmon fishing experience in Iceland. I flew there in the middle of August 1956 in the hope of finding low water and consequently good dry fly fishing. During my two week visit I fished two rivers, the Thvera which flows into the ocean on the west coast, and the Laxa on the north coast, right at the

Arctic Circle. My guide and companion for the two weeks was an attractive young business executive from Reyjavik who had no interest in fishing but who was anxious to earn some foreign exchange for a vacation in Europe.

For the first six days I shared a lease of several miles of the Thvera River with a retired British ambassador named Greenway. The Thvera is a small but lovely stream with clear water and many fine pools. After emerging from a mountain gorge it meanders for miles through open meadows and hay fields. There were plenty of salmon in the river but unfortunately all of them were congregated at the bottom of deep pools.

For the first five days my ambassadorial friend and I threw every kind of wet and dry fly at the salmon without a single strike for either of us. As a matter of fact, I fished myself to the point of exhaustion because, at this latitude, there was plenty of light for fishing until midnight, and I found it difficult to drag myself away from the stream. Meanwhile, Greenway's guide, a member of the Reykjavik fire depart- ment spent his time consuming the ambassador's Scotch whiskey and hauling in a large number of salmon by the use of a plug casting rod and a large spoon.

On the evening of the fifth day I examined the log book in the little cabin where we all slept. To my amazement I discovered that, out of 125 salmon reported killed on that section of the river in 1956 prior to our visit, 119 had been taken on worms and spoons, and only six on flies. The next morning, on my sixth and final day, I decided to abandon my scruples and to try fishing with a bunch of angleworms strung on a large hook.

It was not easy to cast this heavy lure with a fly rod but I managed to toss it into the water at the head of a pool and let it sink deeply and drift down through the length of the pool. The result was startling, to say the least. I killed that day four good grilse, and one 23 pound salmon. In addition, I lost two other good salmon.

That evening, when I returned to the cabin with my catch, Greenway remarked facetiously that he felt he should report my tactics to The Anglers' Club of New York. I replied that, if he wished to remain a purist, and complete his vacation without a single strike (and this is exactly what happened) that was his business and privilege.

For myself, I preferred at least to find out how Icelandic salmon could be taken.

During my entire visit to Iceland, mine were the only single-handed rods that I saw in action. All the Icelanders whom I met expressed astonishment that one would attempt to kill salmon with such light tackle, and almost equal astonishment that a fly could be cast such long distances with so small a rod. The only other fly rods I saw were huge two-handed affairs. The one used by the ambassador was really a "telegraph pole"—15 feet in length and more than one inch in diameter at the butt. For the most part the Icelanders employed plug casting rods and large spoons, or clusters of worms. Except for Greenway and myself, I saw no one attempting to fish with flies.

My experience on the Thvera River in Iceland brought vividly to mind my first encounter with steelhead, exactly 10 years earlier. In August of 1946, I spent two days fishing the Caycuse River which flows to the ocean on the west side of Vancouver Island. My companions were Jack Kellogg, his son Bob, and a retired commissioner of the Royal Canadian Mounted Police who bore the improbable name of Sandys-Wunsch. We reached the Caycuse by a trip on a logging railroad to the crest of the range which runs up the center of the island. We then proceeded on foot down the western slope of the range—a drop of about 1,000 feet—until we reached the river in a forest of virgin Douglas fir trees.

The Caycuse at that time was the most spectacularly beautiful stream I had ever seen. A small stream, it lay between vertical walls of granite 30 to 50 feet high. Our only means of reaching the river was by clambering down the trunk of a fallen tree. Overhead the gigantic Douglas firs reached upward to incredible heights and almost formed an arch over the river.

Fishing the Caycuse proved to be "finger-nail" fishing in a very literal sense. Getting from one pool to another along the base of the granite walls was so difficult that I quickly abandoned my waders and fished in my short under-drawers and a pair of tennis sneakers. On several occasions I found myself holding my rod in my teeth and working my way along the face of the rock, while clinging desperately with my fingers and toes.

Practically every large pool in the river was filled with summer steelhead. Unfortunately, however, they all lay at the bottom of these deep pools and could not be induced to move. For two days we all tried strenuously to sink our wet flies and drag them past the noses of these fish, but none of us had a single strike.

Looking backward from my visit to the Thvera River in Iceland, and my two days on the Caycuse, I can see that both experiences were practically identical. Knowing what I do now about the habits of steelhead and Atlantic salmon, I certainly should have used a wet fly with a small spinner attached, or even a small spoon on these steelhead. With such lures I am confident I would have had instantaneous action. If any had been available, I might even have tried to tempt these fish with a cluster of worms on a hook.

An important aspect of salmon fishing is the necessity of making a delayed strike. You must not strike a salmon as you would any trout, including steelhead, the instant you see the fish swirl at the fly. If you do, you are almost certain either to yank the fly away from the fish or to hook it insecurely in the lip, which means the probable loss of the fish during the ensuing battle. A salmon must be given time to start turning away with the fly in its mouth. A delayed strike at this point will implant the hook firmly in the corner of the fish's jaw. As I found to my sorrow, this is not an easy thing for an experienced trout fisherman to learn, because his reflexes have become so conditioned to an instantaneous strike.

During my first encounter with Atlantic salmon I had no difficulty with a delayed strike. I was one of a party fishing the River of Ponds and Portland Creek in Newfoundland. It was early in August with low water and ideal conditions for dry fly fishing. As a result, practically all of the 16 salmon and grilse that I killed during the five day visit were taken on dry flies. The reason for my success, of course, was that in dry fly fishing there is almost always a good deal of slack line lying on the water. The recovery of this slack gives you an automatic delayed strike, with the lapse of just enough time to permit the fish to start turning away and to get the hook firmly imbedded in its jaw.

Where I really ran into trouble was on the Restigouche River a couple of years later. It was early July with high water and a fairly stiff current. We fished entirely with large wet flies, giving constant action to the lure after a quartering downstream cast. All the fishing was done from large canoes anchored out in the stream. Because of the high water we could not see the salmon, and, as a result, the strike, when it occurred, was usually unexpected.

For the first couple of days I had a very bad time of it. I lost a considerable number of good fish with my instinctive fast strikes, either jerking the fly away from them or losing them later because the fish were insecurely hooked. Gradually, however, I brought my reflexes under control and my record began to improve.

My wife Bobby, with a much more limited background of fly fishing, caught on almost immediately to the delayed strike. Under the stern tutelage of her young Scots Canadian guide named Jimmy Firth, she became a very apt pupil in the art of salmon fishing. She developed her own technique for accomplishing the delayed strike. When a fish hit, she first sat down in the canoe and only then raised the tip of her rod. To my surprise and pleasure, she was the high rod on the river for the week we were there. She killed a 34 pound salmon, six that ran between 20 and 25 pounds, and a great many smaller salmon and grilse.

It is my belief that, in low, clear water, Atlantic salmon are apt to be much less scary than steelhead. I have already reported just how spooky steelhead can be under such conditions. In contrast, I recall vividly one experience with salmon on the River of Ponds. One afternoon I shared a pool with my friend, Charlie Calderini, who had very little experience with a fly rod. Charlie was casting into the pool from the right bank while I was operating from the left bank.

The pool was long and fairly shallow, and contained a large number of boulders which provided excellent holding water for salmon. On every forward cast Charlie's line and fly would hit the water with a big splash. He would then jerk his fly out of the water from the middle of the pool, producing a flash that would have scared any self-respecting steelhead within a radius of at least 50 yards. Meanwhile, I was making every one of my casts as carefully and precisely as possible. The end of the story is that Charlie killed five good grilse that afternoon, and my score was only three. I am confident that, if the pool had contained steelhead instead of salmon, neither of us would have had a single strike.

Before I visited the Skeena Valley I believed that steelhead always ran much smaller in size than Atlantic salmon. The Kispiox steelhead, however, running as they do up to 36 and 40 pounds, convinced me that these fish can be as large as all but a rare few of the Atlantic salmon. The average size of our catch on the Sustut was just about 12 pounds. I am sure that the average size of catches on the Kispiox must be at least 15 pounds.

Such figures compare respectably with the averages for most Atlantic salmon streams, particularly when the many grilse killed are taken into account. Thus, a twenty-year analysis of the salmon catch on a Gaspé river has shown that the average size of these fish, excluding grilse, was just 13 pounds for the entire period.* I also understand that the seventy-year record of the Restigouche Club shows an average weight of salmon taken of just over 17 pounds.† The Restigouche River, just like the Kispiox for steelhead, has the reputation of producing larger salmon than any other stream in North America.

I am fully aware that in discussing the relative fighting qualities of steelhead and Atlantic salmon, I am treading on highly controversial ground. Perhaps any comparisons between these two magnificent game fish should be considered invidious. Both species pack tremendous resources of energy, and both run and jump like wild horses. Nevertheless, I have observed certain minor differences in the action of the two species that I feel are worth recording.

First, it seems to me that the initial strike of a steelhead is likely to be more gentle than that of a salmon. On numerous occasions I have had steelhead suck in dry flies so quietly that I was sure I had hooked a small trout, until I saw the monster erupt from the water a couple of seconds later. On the other hand, during my first encounter with Atlantic salmon in Newfoundland I was surprised by the heaviness of the initial strikes. In fact, I lost a few fish because I was holding

* John E. Hutton: *Trout and Salmon Fishing* — Atlantic, Little Brown 1949, p. 54.
† Dean Witter: *Meanderings of a Fisherman* — p. 57.

the line with my free hand when the strike occurred and the 10 pound test leader snapped like a thread.

Second, I believe that Atlantic salmon are generally more lethargic than steelhead, until they are brought into action by the pull of the line. This would seem to be indicated by the greater spookiness of steelhead in low, clear water. Lee Wulff has written of hooking salmon, and then placing his rod on the ground while setting up his camera, in the confident belief that the fish would rest quietly until aroused. I should hesitate to try this on a steelhead. Also, I have had several large salmon set themselves at the bottom of deep pools and refuse to budge until finally dislodged by rocks tossed into the stream. Doubtless, this has also happened with steelhead, but never in my own experience.

Finally, and admitting it may be a matter of personal prejudice, I must state that I have never felt anything quite like a fresh-run steelhead on the end of my line. The violence and length of the runs and the wild abandon of the jumps produce a spine-tingling effect I have never experienced with any other fish.

Now just a few words in conclusion about the eating qualities of these two fish. For many years I have felt that a baked Atlantic salmon, served cold with a sour cream and cucumber sauce, is the most delicious and delicately flavored fish I have ever tasted. This I still believe. Nevertheless, I have rarely had any better eating than the steelhead steaks broiled by Hunter Simpson for our party on the Sustut River.

IX   *Big Game in The Skeena Valley*

ALTHOUGH THIS IS a story about fishing, it would be incomplete without a brief account of the wild animal life found in the Skeena watershed. At the outset I must confess that I am not much of a big game hunter. I have shot mountain goat, grizzly and black bear, moose and deer, but I find little pleasure any longer in killing these magnificent creatures. I would always enjoy shooting a camp-raiding grizzly, but otherwise I am perfectly content to let my companions obtain the trophies and provide the fresh meat for camp.

The truth is also that I have become too old for the strenuous exercise involved in most big game hunting. In 1954 and 1955, when I was in my middle fifties, I went up three times on foot to the crest of the range above Morice Lake. This was a rugged climb of over 4,000 feet, without benefit of trails, and each time I lugged two big rifles. Now that I have passed sixty I realize it would be unfair to the issuers of my life insurance to undertake any such violent exertion.

For the hunting enthusiast, however, the Skeena Valley offers an ample supply and a wide assortment of big animals. Moose are found throughout the whole area. Mule deer are also widespread but are somewhat scarce as a result of their constant slaughter by timber wolves. Caribou are abundant in the wild northern sections of the watershed. Mountain goat are found on almost every range of mountains but, oddly enough, there are no mountain sheep in the valley. This is strange because just north of the divide, in the watersheds of the Stikine and

Mackenzie Rivers, there are plenty of stone sheep, and still further north one finds the famous Dall sheep.

Grizzly bear and black bear cover the whole watershed, but are particularly abundant in the areas close to the rivers where salmon spawn. Mountain lion are occasionally found. I saw the body of one lion that had just been shot at the edge of the road between Smithers and Hazelton. It was a magnificent specimen, and must have weighed at least 175 pounds. Amongst the smaller fur-bearing animals are lynx, marten, mink, otter, beaver, fox and wolverine. Timber wolves are everywhere, but are especially thick in the northern part of the area.

When I first visited this country I was told that, during World War II, because of the shortage of manpower, the timber wolves practically took over the entire hinterland. Until this plague was brought under control after the war, these fierce predators threatened to exterminate all the moose, caribou and mule deer in the area. I heard numerous tales of moose seeking refuge in the village streets during the winter months. Mountain goat and grizzly bear remained plentiful, however, because the wolves could not reach the goat in their mountain homes, and because no self-respecting wolf would ever tackle an adult grizzly.

I have had no reason to doubt the authenticity of this story, at least as far as the southern part of the watershed is concerned. Goat and grizzly are abundant in the Morice River country but, during my four visits to this area, I saw only one pair of caribou, relatively few moose, and no mule deer. Also, as an indication of the success of the campaign to bring the plague of wolves under control, I never once heard the sound of a wolf, and saw no wolf tracks.

Nevertheless, there was something about this story that always bothered me. Why should the wolves almost succeed in exterminating the other animals during World War II, merely because of the shortage of manpower? If such a development could occur at so recent a period, why had not the same thing taken place many years earlier, before the coming of man? My visit to the Sustut Lake area in 1959 supplied a clue to this conundrum. Here we found moose and caribou in great abundance, and also evidence of a large population of timber wolves. Wolf tracks were everywhere, and on clear nights the sound of wolves was all around us.

What this experience meant to me was that, in wilderness areas virtually untouched by man, Mother Nature usually maintains a normal balance amongst her various wild creatures. If this balance is upset, it is likely to be the result of some activity by Man, the intruder. Thus, I believe that the shortage of manpower during the war years provides an inadequate explanation to account for the plague of wolves at that time. Doubtless, this was part of the story, but I am confident that something else must have occurred prior to the war years that upset the normal balance between the wolves and the other animals. Perhaps the activities of trappers had reduced the number of wolves to a point that permitted the rapid proliferation of the animals on which wolves usually prey. The corollary to this hypothesis would have been a sudden explosion of the wolf population, not only as a result of the cessation of trapping activities during the war, but also because of the abundant food supply available at the beginning of the war period.

The above, of course, represents merely my own rationalization of the problem, and is not based upon any actual knowledge of the facts. It does seem clear to me, however, that some such logic is needed to account for the fact that this sudden upset in the normal wilderness balance took place at this particular time, rather than during the ages prior to the coming of Man.

During my four visits to Morice Lake between 1951 and 1955, my experiences with big game were limited almost entirely to grizzly bear and mountain goat. Occasionally we saw moose swimming across the lake, and once when flying in from Smithers we had a close-up view of a pair of caribou running up the side of a mountain. Mountain goat were all over the high ranges around the lake, and the grizzlies were thick around the river when the salmon were spawning.

During the summer and early fall, prior to salmon spawning, grizzly bear usually remain above the timber line, where they feed chiefly on marmot—a small burrowing animal similar to the prairie dog. When the spawning season arrives, however, they descend en masse to the rivers where they gorge themselves on the dying salmon. Grizzlies are usually much more wary than black bears and are not likely to be seen on river banks before dusk. It is somewhat surprising, therefore, that I have seen a large number of grizzlies on the Morice River, but only a single black bear. Exactly the opposite was true on the Kispiox River where we saw at least ten black bears to every grizzly.

My first glimpse of a grizzly took place during the weekend in September, 1951, when we visited Morice Lake while the salmon were spawning. The hunting party we had met on our arrival spent most of that Saturday lounging around at the head of the river, doing some desultory fishing with plug casting rods, and waiting for the coming of evening. Meanwhile, our party of six was fishing about a quarter of a mile downstream. Several times during the afternoon we heard heavy animals crashing through the undergrowth in the forest immediately behind us, and we were sure that these sounds could be produced only by large bears. I am afraid we found it somewhat difficult to concentrate on our casting, particularly since we had only one rifle amongst the six of us. Finally, just about dusk I saw a large grizzly come out on the bank about 200 yards below us.

In response to our shouts, the hunting party went into immediate action. They came roaring down the river in their boat with the big outboard motor wide open. I shall never forget the sight as they passed us; the hunters crouched around the bow with their rifles at ready, and Jack Nelson standing on an elevated platform in the stern, holding a long tiller in his hand. With his blonde hair flying in the breeze, Jack looked for all the world like a young Viking. The hunters came back up the river about ten p.m., and we learned that they had bagged four grizzlies, one for each member of the party.

Two things one can be certain of regarding grizzlies: they are always unpredictable, and they tend to react violently to the sight or smell of human beings. Usually the reaction takes the form of running away, but one can never be sure. It is always dangerous to stumble unexpectedly upon a grizzly at close range, and it is usually disastrous to get between a female and her cubs. Every bear hunter knows what a frightfully dangerous animal a wounded grizzly can be, particularly because of its ability to absorb large quantities of lead without collapsing. For these reasons, it is not intelligent to travel around in a grizzly bear country, except in the company of an experienced guide armed with a high-powered rifle.

One amusing experience I had with a grizzly on the Morice illustrates the violence of their reactions to human beings. One afternoon I was fishing near the mouth of Gosnell Creek about 10 miles below the lake. I was wading out from the right bank of the river, while my attendant guide, Martin Grainger, reclined on the opposite shore with his rifle beside him. The bank above him rose almost vertically for about 25 feet and then leveled out into a broad, flat shelf covered with coarse gravel.

All at once I caught sight of a big grizzly nosing his way toward the edge of this upper shelf. Since a good breeze was blowing in our direction he was not yet aware of our presence. Suddenly the bear looked up and saw me. In a flash he wheeled like a polo pony and dashed off into the forest. His reaction was so sudden that his paws threw up a shower of loose gravel which rained down on Martin directly below. To say that my guide was startled would be an understatement.

When I went into Morice Lake in August 1954, in the company of Hal Hentz and Hunter Perry, I had acquired for the first time a hunting license. I did this chiefly on the chance of shooting a grizzly on the river while fishing. The idea of climbing the ranges in pursuit of goat had not entered my mind. These ranges, rising as they did from 3,500 to 4,500 feet above the lake, looked too formidable for a middle-aged business man from the city.

Late one afternoon, however, when the setting sun shone brilliantly on the range directly opposite our camp, Martin Grainger announced that he could see a big goat right at the crest. With powerful binoculars we quickly verified what Martin had seen with his bare eyes. Since the lake was two miles wide at this point, and the crest over 4,000 feet above the lake and at least two miles back from the shore, Martin's eyesight seemed extraordinary. On the spur of the moment I decided it would be fun to climb the range after the goat, and Martin and Barry Grainger agreed to accompany me.

We set out the next morning at eight, the guides carrying sleeping bags, a canvas lean-to, and food supplies for two days, and I carrying two 30-06 rifles. We reached the timber line around noon, about 500 feet below the crest. Here we made camp and had a bite of lunch. Early in the afternoon we resumed our climb. Just as we emerged from behind a high spur of rock we spotted a large grizzly digging in the ground after grubs or marmot. We quickly slid behind the rock spur in an attempt to move around to the left behind the bear. The latter, evidently sensing our presence, moved off slowly to the right. We came out into the open just in time to see the grizzly disappear behind a low ledge of rock. We dropped to our hands and knees and began to crawl slowly forward. About half a minute later the grizzly's head and shoulders appeared from behind the opposite side of the ledge, and about 250 yards distant. There he stood absolutely immobile watching us intently while we froze to the ground. Unable to stand the strain for long I finally decided to shoot. Slowly raising my rifle I aimed for a spot about six inches above the bear's right shoulder to allow for the drop of my 220 grain bullet. When I squeezed the trigger the grizzly fell back out of sight obviously hit.

We then jumped to our feet and ran forward. When we came around the ledge we found the bear back on his feet, and standing as though dazed and not yet comprehending what had happened. As soon as he saw us, however, the grizzly dashed off at high speed on three legs, with his right foreleg dangling limply at his side. It was clear my heavy bullet had broken the bear's right shoulder but had not found a vital spot. All three of us fired running shots without apparent effect just before the grizzly disappeared over the side of the mountain into the heavy bush. It seemed a shame to abandon the pursuit of a badly wounded animal, but Barry soon convinced me that it would be worse than useless to follow the bear down the mountain. He was certain that the bear, even with a broken shoulder, could travel for miles without collapsing.

Resuming our climb we soon reached the crest of the range at exactly the spot where we had seen the goat the evening before. Just as we came over the crest we spotted the big Billy goat slightly below and not more than 100 yards distant. It was standing watching us, not more than 15 feet from the edge of a precipice which had a sheer drop of at least 2,000 feet. I raised my rifle and fired, but the goat stood stock still and gave no apparent sign of having been hit. I quickly slammed a second shell into the chamber and was just squeezing the trigger when the goat took one tremendous leap forward. To the surprise of all of us, it collapsed, stone dead, not more than three feet from the edge of the abyss. We discovered later that my first shot had gone right through the animal's heart and had come out on the other side.

This was the biggest and fattest mountain goat I have ever seen. Its horns measured exactly 11 inches which I understood was just under a record. It had a gargantuan belly and must have weighed at least 250 pounds. Because of the huge girth the hide made a beautiful rug which still adorns my home.

Next fall, in September of 1955, I made two more trips to the crest of the range, accompanied by George Bates and my 17-year-old son, Dick. George and I had some long-distance shots at goats, at ranges between 400 and 500 yards, but neither of us connected. Dick was the only one of us who succeeded in bagging a goat. He shot this animal at 7:30 in the morning in a driving sleet storm. It had rained heavily during the night, and by morning the rain had turned to sleet, which was driven into our faces by a strong wind. The goat, when hit, rolled some 600 feet down a steep rock slide. While Dick and the guides scrambled down to skin out the goat I remained on the crest. The sleet cut my face, and I was drenched to the skin through my rain parka. I have never been so cold and miserable in my life.

Strange as it may seem, a female skunk provided considerable pleasure and amusement for us during two successive visits to Morice Lake. When we reached the lake in August of 1953, we found this small animal living in a large hollow log on the shore right in front of our camp. At first the near presence of this terrifying creature made us somewhat apprehensive. We soon discovered, however, that she was entirely friendly and minded her own business as long as we minded ours. Moreover, she remained entirely odorless during her lengthy stay in our camp. Just to insure friendly relations we frequently left a pan of milk at one end of the log when we retired at night. In the morning we always found the milk consumed and our little friend snuggled back in the recesses of her wooden home.

On my return to Morice Lake the following fall I was delighted to find the skunk still occupying the same old log. Everything went well

Hide of huge grizzly shot by Charlie Calderini in Kispiox Valley

Ron Sanderson with bull caribou which he shot on range above Sustut Lake

Davey Bob, Indian guide, surveying devastation of Sustut Lake camp by a grizzly bear

for about ten days, with mutual respect and goodwill displayed on both sides. Then, on two successive nights, our guides awakened to find the little creature nosing around inside their tent. They lay absolutely still until she departed, but the strain on their nerves was too great to endure. The second morning Martin Grainger found the skunk some distance away from the log and reached for his rifle. The little animal had never previously shown any fear of us, but immediately the rifle appeared she bolted for the woods. Unfortunately, Martin's bullet was too fast for her, and ended the saga of our friendly skunk.

My next experience with big game in the Skeena Valley was in the fall of 1959. As previously recounted, I spent the first two weeks of September on the Upper Kispiox River, and the balance of the month in the area of Sustut Lake and Johanson Lake. Our party on the Kispiox consisted of Charlie Calderini, Bob Fisher, Tom Cassady, and myself. We spent the entire fortnight at Jack Lee's Corral Creek Camp, about five miles below the junction of Sweetin Creek with the Kispiox. Calderini and Fisher were the hunters of our party, while Cassady and I were interested primarily in fishing. Nevertheless, because the fishing was so poor, I did accompany my hunting companions on several of their excursions after moose and bear.

The humpback salmon were spawning all over the river at the time and scarcely a day passed that we failed to see one or more black bears. Since there is no game limit on black bear, Charlie and Bob bagged several of these animals. The grizzlies proved much more elusive, however, and rarely came down to the river before dusk. Jack Lee had planted a dead horse for bear bait at a likely spot near the river, and Bob Fisher spent numerous evenings in ambush at this place waiting for grizzlies to appear. On two separate occasions he spotted a big grizzly approaching the bait and fired in the semi-darkness. Each time the bear was knocked down, but managed to roll out of sight in the shadows and disappear. On each of the following mornings Bob and Jack Lee followed the blood trails of these wounded animals for several miles before they lost them.

Just before dusk on the evening before my departure for Sustut Lake, Charlie Calderini was riding in a jeep truck with Bill Love at the wheel. Bill is the brother of our guide, Wally, but is not a licensed guide himself. About a mile below our camp they spotted a huge grizzly some 200 yards back from the road. Stopping the truck, they both jumped out and started toward the grizzly. As the bear turned to look at them, Charlie fired and hit the animal directly between the eyes, killing it instantly. After putting a second shot in the grizzly's neck for safety, Charlie turned around and noticed that Bill, in his excitement, had left his rifle behind in the truck.

Charlie is a magnificent shot, both with a rifle and a shotgun, and is an experienced big game hunter, although he had never pursued grizzly bear before this trip. Prior to this incident, Calderini had told us on several occasions that the one thing he insisted upon in grizzly hunting was to be covered at all times by an armed and experienced guide. Of course, he was right, but it was ironic for him to bag this huge grizzly and then discover that the amateur guide beside him was wholly unarmed. Charlie told me afterward that the experience did not bother him until he woke up in the middle of that night, and suddenly broke out in a cold sweat thinking about the possibilities.

This particular grizzly was almost a record for the area. It measured 8 feet, 6 inches from the tip of its nose to the end of its stubby tail, and must have weighed somewhere around 800 pounds. Surprisingly, it was almost coal black in color. I had never heard of black grizzlies before, but discovered in an article after my return to the States that such color is not uncommon in these animals.

Moose hunting was done in broad daylight, and I accompanied my friends on several of these excursions both on foot and on horseback. The rutting season had not yet started, and the moose, especially the bulls, were lying very low. It was extraordinary to me how these huge and awkward looking animals could move so silently and conceal themselves so effectively. Fresh moose signs were everywhere but the moose themselves proved almost as elusive as timber wolves. Time and again we came upon beds in the high grass which had just been vacated by moose on our approach. Once we followed the tracks of a big bull for several miles along a game trail. The tracks were so fresh that the water in the huge hoof prints was still muddy. When we finally gave up and turned back we found the moose had doubled around and was preceding us back down the same trail.

Probably the moose were unusually wary because of the heavy execution during the previous hunting season. Jack Lee told us that, during the fall of 1958, the first season after the extension of the road to Sweetin Creek, more than 70 moose had been shot in the Upper Kispiox Valley. That these animals were still in plentiful supply, how' ever, was indicated by the vast number of moose signs that we found. Of course, when the rutting season is on, and the bulls are running, they are much easier to spot and to shoot.

Nevertheless, none of us saw a single moose until the day before the end of our visit. On that occasion, Bob Fisher finally caught up with and killed a fine bull. The animal had a magnificent rack of horns, with a spread of 54 inches.

When I joined my three Canadian friends and flew into Sustut Lake on September 14th, we found the surrounding country a paradise for big game hunters. Moose and caribou were in abundant supply, and grizzly bear were all over the area. We spotted goat on almost every mountain range, and everywhere we went we saw signs of timber wolves. One afternoon Buzz Fiorini flew out to Babine to bring in some fresh supplies. On his way back he reported counting five separate herds of caribou. We frequently saw moose feeding along the shores of Sustut Lake and of the lower bay.

I attempted no shooting on this trip although I had several excellent opportunities to kill moose if I had cared to do so. The most interesting of these experiences took place one morning when I went down by myself to fish the pool just above the lower bay of Sustut Lake. To my surprise I saw two low black mounds protruding out of the shallow water of the bay about 200 yards distant. Since I had no recollection of seeing any such mounds on my previous trips to this spot, I rubbed my eyes and looked again. Just then two huge heads emerged from the water—a big bull moose and a cow moose, feeding on the bottom of the bay.

At the sight of me the bull started to move slowly toward the shore on the left while the cow kept right on feeding. The bull came out on the bank and stood for several minutes watching me nervously. He finally turned away and disappeared into the forest. The cow, on the other hand, not only remained entirely unconcerned by my presence, but actually worked her way slowly in my direction. By the time I broke off fishing and started back upstream she was less than 100 yards away.

It is highly improbable that these animals had ever been shot at, and I hate to think that the female of the species was merely the braver of the two. Yet somehow the bull recognized a potential enemy in me at once, and realized that he should vacate his highly vulnerable position. The cow, on the other hand, seemed to feel perfectly safe, and actually gave me the impression of being relieved when her boy friend decided to take a powder.

My companions took enough time off from fishing to have some excellent hunting. Ron Sanderson shot a fine bull caribou and a goat on one of the ranges above Sustut Lake, while Buzz Fiorini also got a goat on the same expedition. Brian Magee shot another goat near the top of a mountain beside Johanson Lake. As a result, we had an ample supply of fresh meat in camp, at least until a grizzly bear stole it all right from under our noses.

GRIZZLIES IN CAMP

In an earlier chapter brief mention was made of the devastation of our camp on Sustut Lake by a marauding grizzly. The incident was unusual enough to justify telling in some detail. When we flew back to Sustut from Johanson Lake, we found our tent torn to shreds, our luggage chewed to pieces and our belongings scattered over the landscape. It really looked as though the bear, in its frustration at not finding any food, had taken pleasure in destroying everything in sight.

When I finally gathered my scattered possessions, practically the only items unmarked by the bear's teeth were $800 in traveler's checks, and my airline ticket back to Chicago. When Ron Sanderson saw these, he remarked: "Jesus, John, that was a stupid bear."

"What do you mean?" I asked.

"Well," said Ron, "if he had had half a grain of sense, he would have taken the ticket and money, and would now be on his way to see the World Series in Chicago."

That same afternoon, Gus Craig, Ron Sanderson, Buzz Fiorini, and Davey Bob, one of our Indian guides, trekked down to the junction of the Sustut with Johanson Creek. Brian Magee and I remained at Sustut Lake, accompanied by Hunter Simpson, our white cook and Dominic Abrahams, our other Indian. Brian and I occupied the remnants of the main tent, while Hunter and Dominic slept under a canvas fly about 20 feet away.

That evening we all speculated as to the possibility of a return visit from the bear. I thought it highly improbable with human beings in camp. Nevertheless, I remained awake for hours listening for the grizzly. Several times around one a.m., I thought I heard the sound of snapping twigs but was never sure enough to go outside and investigate. About an hour later the stillness of the night was shattered by the crash of Hunter Simpson's 30-06 rifle. Brian and I grabbed our rifles and dashed out of the tent. We discovered that Hunter had fired at the shadowy form of the grizzly on its *second* visit that night to our camp.

The bear had come into camp around one a.m., had walked up to within five feet of Hunter's head, and picked up in its fore paws a floppy cardboard box containing about 40 pounds of fresh caribou and goat meat. Dominic woke up just in time to see the huge grizzly walking off on its hind legs like a man, towering more than eight feet in height, and carrying the box in its fore paws. As we discovered the next morning, the bear carried the box about 200 yards off into the forest, where it sat down and devoured the entire contents.

The grizzly then paid us a second visit about two a.m., and was chewing on one of our goat hides when Hunter shot at it. In retrospect it was probably very fortunate that Hunter did not hit the bear. A wounded grizzly in total darkness could have been a frightful animal. It could have been on top of us before we even saw it. The bear disappeared into the darkness and never returned again. The crash of the big rifle probably startled it even more than it did us.

The next morning found us really short of solid food, a deficit that Brian and I overcame by catching several good steelhead trout. The rest of the day we spent in making preparations for the anticipated visit of the bear that night. First, we lashed a 15 pound cohoe salmon to a tree. Second, we filled a bunch of empty cans with pebbles and strung them on a cord at strategic points around the tree, so that if the bear bumped against the cord a first class racket would ensue. Third, each member of the group was shown how to hold a flashlight in his left hand under the barrel of his rifle in the method used in jacklighting deer. Finally, I attached one end of a fly line to my wrist and the other end to Hunter Simpson's wrist, with the understanding that the first one to hear the bear would yank the line three times. Of course, the grizzly never reappeared, although we stayed awake most of the night waiting for it.

While all of this was taking place, the other members of our party had an encounter with another grizzly at the Junction camp. When they arrived they found the tent there also torn to shreds. Since practically nothing had been left in the tent no further damage had been done. That evening they all lay awake listening for the return of their grizzly.

About midnight Davey Bob announced quietly that he could hear a bear splashing across the river a short distance below the camp. A few moments later they all heard the grizzly moving slowly through the heavy undergrowth about 50 feet away. At this point Gus Craig whispered to Davey to empty his rifle into the air in an effort to frighten the animal away, and this was done. Immediately thereafter the big animal crashed off through the brush and splashed back across the river. The grizzly never reappeared.

The next morning the group was surprised to find Davey Bob stacking big piles of firewood at various points around the camp. When they asked what he was doing, Davey replied: "Going to build fires tonight—keep big bear away."

When they tried to kid him about this, Davey said, "You laugh— big bear come in tent; go wham, wham, wham (making the motions of a boxer throwing left and right hooks)—everybody dead—better we all go home. My brother slapped in face by grizzly—no face left."

These experiences, together with the genuine terror displayed by our Indians, gave me increased respect for grizzly bears, and the serious menace they can be to camping parties. In all probability these bears had had no previous contact with humans, and undoubtedly they were very hungry. Otherwise, I doubt very much that they would have been so bold as to come right into occupied camps. Nevertheless, the fact that they did demonstrates the necessity for eternal vigilance when camping out in a grizzly bear country.

I should also like to emphasize that our Indian guides were not the cigar store variety of Indian. They were genuine wilderness Indians, members of the Carrier tribe, and both made their living by trapping and hunting. The one animal they feared was the grizzly bear, and they made no effort to conceal this terror.

What kind of a rifle should one use for grizzly bear? On countless occasions hunters have demonstrated that, if hit in a vital spot, a grizzly can be killed with a rifle as small as a 30-30 caliber. These were the weapons used by both of our Indian guides; probably because of their lightness and inexpensiveness. The problem, of course, is to hit a grizzly in a vital spot. The standard weapon used by most of the white guides is the 30-06 rifle. This is a powerful gun and packs enough shocking power to stop most grizzlies.

Nevertheless, I have now seen too many examples of grizzlies getting away after having been knocked down by a 30-06 bullet. Shortly after our departure from the Kispiox, Jack Lee wrote Bob Fisher that he had just shot a grizzly which absorbed seven 30-06 slugs before it was killed. Partly for safety and partly because I hate to see badly wounded animals get away, I am now inclined to believe that an even more powerful weapon is desirable. I have recently acquired a Browning 338 magnum rifle which I shall take with me when I return to northern British Columbia. It is a beautiful piece of machinery and packs a shocking power more than 40 percent greater than a 30-06. Its ballistics show a muzzle energy of over 4,000 foot pounds with a 250 grain bullet. This compares with approximately 2,800 foot pounds of shocking power for a 30-06 with a 220 grain bullet.

I intend to tape a powerful flashlight to the barrel of this weapon. Thus equipped I hope to be ready for any camp raiding grizzly. If I can't kill a grizzly with a Browning 338 perhaps I should follow Davey Bob's advice when he said: "Better we all go home."

X *Epilogue*

SINCE THE DAYS of Isaak Walton a well established tradition has dictated that every book on fishing include some paean of praise to the joys of the art of the angle. In all probability this is the only volume on the subject I shall ever attempt to write. As a consequence, I feel the urge to put down on paper a brief account of what fly fishing has meant to me.

Like many other sports, the art of fly fishing can be mastered more easily if one has had the good fortune to learn the fundamentals in early childhood. Somewhat unfortunately for myself, my interest in fly fishing began fairly late in life, and as a result of a deliberate decision. During World War II, when I was in my middle forties, I spent three years as a bureaucrat in Washington. Like countless others in war service at that time my mind frequently revolved around the subject of the things I would like to do after the end of the war. Golf had been my chief outdoor hobby during all of my adult years, and at one time I had played with a very low handicap. Unfortunately, I could see no satisfactory future for my golf game. I realized that, with each passing year, my long shots would become shorter, and my handicap would rise progressively with my age.

What fun it would be to find a new hobby at which I could see improvement rather than deterioration as the years passed, and which I could enjoy virtually as long as I could stand on two feet! After considering several other possibilities I finally concluded that fly fishing might be the answer to my prayer. First, it would give me an outdoor life which I loved in almost any form. Second, it would furnish as much physical exercise as might be suitable for any particular stage of life. Finally, I realized that it was an art that required delicacy of skill rather than brute strength, and the possibilities of which could never be exhausted no matter how proficient one might become.

I am afraid that my early efforts were quite pathetic. I discovered that learning the art of fly fishing is something very different from learning other sports. You cannot just go to your club and take regular lessons from a professional, as you do in golf or tennis. You may practice casting on your lawn, as I have done hundreds of times, but you will never really learn anything about fly fishing until you get out on a stream and try doing it yourself.

Once you are on the stream, you will be very fortunate if you find an expert fisherman who is willing to instruct you in the fundamentals of the art. A father will usually do this for a son, but most ex-perienced anglers are too busy with their own fishing to waste time on an adult tyro. Although I have found some valuable and heartwarming exceptions to this rule, I had to learn largely by the slow process of trial and error, and by picking up odd bits of knowledge from an observation of others.

My original equipment was just about as shabby as my ability to handle it. Gradually, however, both my equipment and my skill began to improve, but at least five years of sporadic angling elapsed before I achieved even a fair grasp of the fundamentals of fly fishing. I remember vividly my first visit to the Sun River in Montana, one of the finest rainbow trout streams in the United States. After two weeks of steady and strenuous angling, my total catch was not more than a dozen trout. Now, I count it a poor day on this stream when I fail to land twenty or more good rainbows on barbless hooks.

Reading about fishing is somewhat like casting on the lawn. It is not of much use to a beginner, but becomes progressively more valuable as your actual experience on streams enables you to understand the finer points of the art. As the years passed, I found myself acquiring a small library of books by the masters of fly fishing, such as Hewitt, La Branche, Bergman, Haig-Brown, Steel, Wulff, and numerous others.

In addition to the pleasure and solace which these volumes afford a fisherman on cold winter nights, they can also add greatly to his store of knowledge.

Amongst the more valuable pointers that I have gleaned from reading rather than from actual stream experience, I would list the following: the necessity for, and methods of stalking fish as you would any other wild creature; the various curve and "slack line" casts; the fun of using spiders in place of ordinary dry flies; the proper use of artificial nymphs, and how to tell that a "bulging trout" is feeding on live nymphs just beneath the surface, rather than taking flies on top of the water; an understanding of the great variety of fly hatches that appear on trout streams. I could continue this list almost indefinitely, but the above should suffice to make the point that reading can be an important supplement to actual experience on a stream.

Now, after more than 18 years of learning. I can look back and ask myself if the rewards from fly fishing have been as great as my anticipations during World War II. The answer is not only strongly affirmative, but in addition there have been some unexpected rewards which now seem at least as important as those I had hoped for.

First amongst these I would place the friendships I have made on many streams in various parts of the world. Genuine friends are much easier to acquire in childhood than in middle age. Largely because of their rarity, real friendships formed in later life tend to become so much the more precious.

Early in my fishing career I discovered that a strong bond of brother-hood exists amongst fly fishermen. With rare exceptions I have found them to be genuine sportsmen who fish for pleasure rather than for meat. The competitive aspect of fishing tends to be subordinated to the pleasure of swapping information and various bits of fishing lore with brother anglers. They share in common a love of the wilderness, the exhilaration that comes from swiftly flowing water, and the surrounding beauty of green forests and snow capped mountains. Finally, in most ardent fly fishermen will be found a streak of poetry and a philosophic approach to the problems of life.

Looking backwards, I think first of Alden Little, retired executive secretary of the Investment Bankers Association. Alden and I fished many western streams together at a time when I scarcely knew the difference between a wet and a dry fly. An enthusiastic angler and a delightful companion, he was my first instructor in the fundamentals of fly fishing. Although he has now become too old to wade streams, Alden will always be one of the fondest memories of my fishing career.

Next I think of Jack Kellogg, who took up my instruction where Alden Little left off. Jack is a first rate fisherman, a fine sportsman, and a keen observer of everything around him on a stream or in the woods. We have had many wonderful experiences fishing together in British Columbia.

I turn now to the numerous good friends I first met on the Sun River in Montana. First, there are Dan Volkmann and Bill Miller of San Francisco. Dan is undoubtedly the most graceful and artistic wielder of a fly rod I have ever seen in action. From the kindness of his heart he gave up many valuable hours of his own on the stream in order to teach me how to handle a rod, and the proper method of casting a dry fly. For this I shall be eternally grateful. Bill Miller has been Dan's boon companion on every stream from the South Island of New Zealand to northern British Columbia, is himself a fine fisherman, and a wonderful companion under any and all circumstances.

Then there is Bill Oliver of Pittsburgh, with whom I have spent many happy days fishing and camping on the Sun River. Bill is a man who reads Keats by flashlight in his sleeping bag at night, and by day is one of the most expert dry fly fishermen I have ever known. To Bill Oliver I am deeply indebted for much that I have learned about the handling of a dry fly.

Charlie Smyth, distinguished professor of chemistry at Princeton, is another good friend with whom I have fished the Sun River in Montana and the Morice River in British Columbia. Charlie delivers lectures, even to the Russians in Moscow, on such esoteric subjects as "The Physics of Dielectrics", and maintains his sanity by an equally passionate devotion to fly fishing. Quiet to the point of self-effacement, Charlie is a great companion on any stream.

Next come the heavenly twins of fly fishing, Hal Hentz and Hunter Perry. Retired widowers, who grew up together in Atlanta, Hal and Hunter spend all their vacations fishing together anywhere in the world from Spain to Alaska. I first met them on the Sun River but also had the good fortune to spend three weeks with them in northern British Columbia. Never have I known two finer gentlemen, or more delightful companions. Hal Hentz is also one of the nation's leading experts on camellias, and spends his spare time in judging camellia shows, and in lecturing on the subject.

Smith Richardson, retired chairman of Vick Chemical Company, is another close friend whom I met first on the Sun River. In addition, he was a member of our party on the trip to northern British Columbia in 1955. A rugged individualist and great sportsman, Smith would rather fish than make money. As one would expect, he bore a recent severe illness with great fortitude, and still spends his summers on the Sun River.

Ed Hilliard of Louisville, southern gentleman of the old school, stands high in the list of fishermen I am proud to call friends. Ed and his lovely wife, Nanine, have been annual guests at the K-Bar-L Ranch on the Sun River for about 30 years. Ed is an expert fly fisherman and loves the wilderness as much as anyone I have ever known. Also, he has done a great deal to preserve good trout fishing on the Sun River. By the force of his personality he has persuaded every ranch guest to use barbless hooks, and return the fish to the stream.

On the occasion of Ed's 73rd birthday at the ranch I wrote the following jingle:

> "You are young, Father Edward," the old
>   man said,
> "Though your hair is whiter than snow,
>   For you romp through these hills like a
>   newlywed.
>   Pray, what is it makes you go?"
>
> "In my youth," said the sage, "I took to
>   the stream.
>   And followed each trout with my wife.
>   The vigor and strength that came from
>   Nanine,
>   Have lasted the rest of my life."

Next on the list are the three good Canadian friends with whom I have made my two latest visits to the Skeena Valley—Albert (Gus) Craig, Brian Magee, and Ron Sanderson. All three are fine sportsmen and wonderful companions in the wilderness. Born in Alaska and educated at Cornell University, Gus Craig has spent most of his adult life in Canada. He is a fine fly fisherman and has pursued trout all over Canada. Brian Magee and Ron Sanderson were relatively inexperienced in handling a fly rod on our first visit to the Skeena. Both, however, have made remarkably rapid progress in the art. On our trip in the fall of 1961, Brian landed more steelhead on dry flies than the combined total for the rest of the party. Ron Sanderson contributed immeasurably to the pleasure of our trips with his inexhaustible fund of humor as we warmed ourselves internally as well as externally in the cold evenings around our campfires.

Last, but not least, I must pay a well-deserved tribute to my wife, Bobby. Poor girl, she had the misfortune of sharing a fishing honeymoon with me on the Sun River. With very little experience at fly fishing, she struggled heroically at the task of learning. Despite the loss of ten pounds in the process, Bobby ended by catching almost as many trout as I did. The next year, on the Restigouche River in New Brunswick, she was the undisputed champion of our camp in killing Atlantic salmon.

While writing of friends, I cannot overlook many of the guides who have accompanied me on various excursions into the wilderness. With one or two exceptions, who shall be nameless, I have found these men to be the salt of the earth. They are simple, fine human beings who, if treated like friends rather than like employees, will usually respond with a devotion that is highly rewarding.

Of the many fine guides I have known, there are two who stand out in my memory above all others. The first is Jack Nelson, head guide of our Morice River trips. Jack was educated at the University of British Columbia, served as a lieutenant in the Canadian Navy during World War II, and then took up guiding because of his love of the wilderness. Gentle, competent and courageous, Jack was described by John Harlan as "one of nature's true gentlemen". I would as willingly entrust my life in Jack Nelson's hands as anyone I have ever met.

Buzz Fiorini cannot properly be classified as a guide. A better description would be that of a professional "white hunter". Buzz organizes hunting and fishing trips, hires and supervises the guides, and even flies his own float plane as an important adjunct to these trips. Buzz is an expert and enthusiastic big game hunter and fly fisherman. With a small, compact frame, he is as strong as a young bull and is tireless on a trail. Buzz Fiorini is at all times a most pleasant and helpful companion in the woods.

Another unexpected reward I discovered in fly fishing is the pleasure one finds merely in the manipulation of the rod and the fly. There is something artistically satisfying in making a long cast and seeing the fly light in exactly the spot and in the manner one planned. Any fisherman who tells you he does not care much whether or not he catches fish is a hypocrite and a liar. Nevertheless, I have fished for days without a strike and still managed to have a good time in the process.

I have none of the instincts of a real naturalist. With my bookish background, my reactions are too cerebral to permit me to be an acute observer of the surrounding flora and fauna. Yet there are compensations for a mind that turns inward. As the brain relaxes and the nerves unravel from the tensions of a modern urban existence, long thoughts come pouring in. Verses from my favorite poets crowd into my mind: verses from Housman, Santayana, Keats, and others whom I have learned to love over the years. Hours slip by, and I am scarcely aware of the passage of time.

Admittedly there is an important element of escapism in my devotion to fly fishing and love of the woods. My urge to escape from big city life, however, is of a qualified nature. It is very different from that of Edwin Arlington Robinson's "Miniver Cheevy", who "cursed the day that he'd been born", and longed for a return of the Middle Ages. Life on the whole has been very kind to me, and probably I should not be happy if permanently removed from the excitement of our megalopolitan civilization.

Nevertheless, there is so much that is unattractive and distasteful about modern living in a big city that I feel the urge to escape to a simpler existence whenever circumstances permit. Besides, I have studied and taught too much history and economics to be an optimist about the future of our civilization and the prospects for survival of our democratic way of life.

In the city I work under the high tensions of the investment banking business, and I have found nothing comparable to a wilderness trout stream to provide relief from these strains. Certainly there is no genuine rest or relaxation for me in the atmosphere of a fashionable resort, with its constant round of cocktail parties and gay night life.

Riches are always a matter of relativity. A man is wealthy in my book if he has sufficient resources within himself to enjoy the simple pleasures of life, and live well within the limits of moderate circumstances. Thus, if his tastes and material desires are simple enough, one individual with a small capital may actually be wealthier than another who has several millions, but who feels compelled to spend more and more in lavish living as his fortune increases.

Luckily, both my wife and I have fairly simple tastes and enjoy hobbies that provide important resources within ourselves. She loves to paint, and I love to read, to write—and to fish. As a result, we would greatly prefer to spend most of our time in some lovely, remote spot than we would in the eternal struggle to keep up with the Joneses. We are now searching for such a hideout in anticipation of the day—we hope not too distant—when I shall be able to take more and more time off from the demanding tempo of my business.

One problem bothers me every year when I start making plans for a fishing trip. I find myself always torn between the thrill of pursuing big game fish like steelhead or Atlantic salmon, and the quieter pleasure of fishing for smaller trout in a stream like the Sun River. It is hard to match the excitement of hooking and battling a huge stream fish, but I am sure that greater skill is usually required in snaring a two or three pound rainbow or brown trout. As time passes, I am afraid that my inclinations will veer more and more to small trout fishing. To handle a small, light rod with a long leader tapered down to 5 x or 6 x, and to place a dry fly or spider in exactly the spot you wish, is probably the quintessence of fly fishing. Or, perhaps, this is just another sign that I am growing old.

When I was fifty the years ahead still seemed to stretch away indefinitely into the future. Now that I have passed sixty I am suddenly aware that only a limited number of fishing seasons remain for me to enjoy. Inevitably the day will arrive when I shall be too old to wade in streams. Meanwhile I cherish each season as a miser hoards his small stock of gold, trying always to keep in mind the words of Aeneas, when he said in a somewhat different context:

"Forsan et haec olim meminisse iuvabit."

And perhaps some day it shall please us to remember these things.

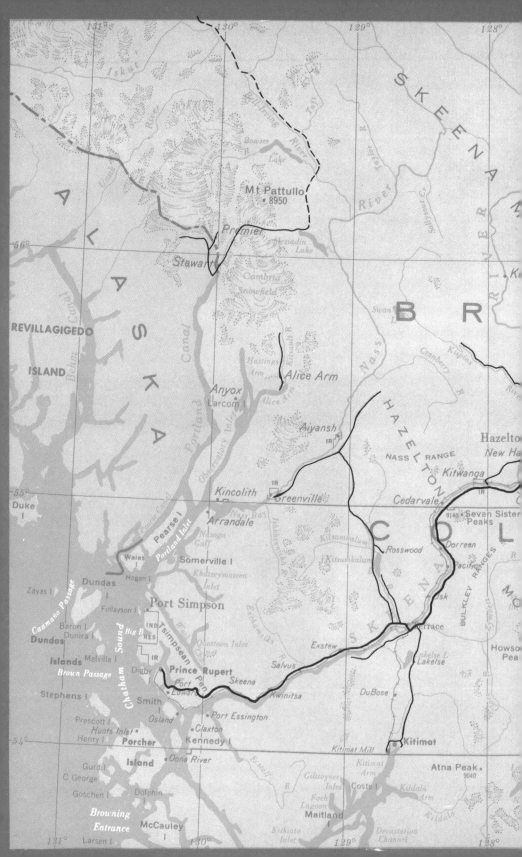